MIRACLES IN MANHATTAN

Stories of Hope and Faith from the Heart of New York City

Compiled by

RON LEWIS

MIRACLES IN MANHATTAN

Quantity sales special discounts are available on quantity purchases by corporations, associations, and others. For details, contact the publisher at the address above.

Orders by U.S. and Canada trade bookstores and wholesalers.
Email info@BeyondPublishing.net

The Beyond Publishing Speakers Bureau can bring authors to your live event. For more information or to book an event contact the Beyond Publishing Speakers Bureau speak@BeyondPublishing.net

The Author can be reached directly at BeyondPublishing.net

Manufactured and printed in the United States of America distributed globally by BeyondPublishing.net

New York | Los Angeles | London | Sydney

ISBN Softcover: 978-1-637921-07-4

ISBN Hardcover: 978-1-637921-19-7

CONTENTS

ACKNOWLEDGEMENTS

A book like this is the result of collaboration between a team of enthusiasts who believe in the value of every person and each story told.

Molly Ford, along with Kaz Iinuma, you have led a wonderful team of volunteer writers and editors, devoting hours of time and talent so that each story rings true with integrity and passion for writer and reader alike. Caleb Galaraga, you have invested in this project as your own from the start, bringing skill, brilliance, and leadership to an extraordinary task.

Peter Ahlin, Eric Syfrett, Shino Prater and Ailsa and Nathan Lewis, your heart to read, write, and serve this process made a daunting task less so. Jennifer Jeanneret you were masterful. A special heartfelt thank-you to Chartwell Literary Group and to Michael Butler and the Beyond Publishing team for inspiring us and pulling it all together.

To the "early responders" who left the comforts of other cities to come into New York in a great moment of need: Adam and Susan, Dave and Chris, Richelle, Bruce and Teri, Lara, Megan, Kevin and Kelly, David and Kathleen E., David and Kathleen W., David and Nadia (so many Davids!), Ron and Hillary, Bryan and Becca, Mabel and Jun, and George and Tondra, we honor your pioneering spirit and unwavering faith.

To the Every Nation, New York City pastoral team and staff, past and present, you have invested so much time helping those who were lost, healing the broken, and building a Christ-centered community as a refuge for our city. You are the common thread behind each story; your labor and care are of eternal value. There would be no book like this without you.

To Lynette Lewis, for years of prayer, devotion, and countless hours of story development in this book, we owe you a debt of gratitude. Your courage and faith have made a difference for so many.

For our storytellers, you who boldly and beautifully share your personal stories, we thank you for your transparency and timeless testimony. You have overcome much, and we are grateful you so boldly tell of the miraculous work of God *in* you and *for* you.

For the many who shared your miracle stories but time and space do not permit your inclusion this time, we eagerly await Volume Two.

There are so many others....It is impossible to mention everyone who had a part in this book, but please know you are not forgotten. Even if you are not mentioned by name, God remembers, records and rewards. This is all for Him.

Finally, and most importantly, it is only through the power of God and the gospel of Jesus Christ that miracle stories like these can happen and be told. All glory belongs to Him alone for each and every miracle in Manhattan, now and forevermore.

FOREWORD

By Darryl Strawberry

I was just 21 years of age when I first came to New York. The cellar-dwelling Mets drafted me #1 straight out of high school, and after I spent a few years learning the ropes in the minor leagues, they called me up to play baseball at Shea Stadium.

My rise to fame and acclaim was unbelievable. Hitting home runs and stealing bases with equal facility, I was named *National League Rookie of the Year* for the 1983 season. Baseball pundits described my swing as one of the most beautiful they had ever seen, comparing me to Ted Williams.

I helped lead the 1986 Mets to a World Series victory, including a game-securing home run in the eighth inning of Game Seven; that was my first of four World Series titles with New York teams. I was an eight-time All Star, appeared on the cover of *Sports Illustrated* seven times, and received a then-astronomical $20 million contract in 1990.

I had everything—but I had nothing.

The childhood abuse I suffered at the hands of my father cast a long shadow over me, his beatings delivering the message that I would never amount to anything. Even baseball success led me to self-destruction, as growing addictions to alcohol, cocaine, amphetamines, and womanizing failed to mend the desperate brokenness I felt inside.

These addictions and their complications led to all kinds of legal trouble, and one day I traded my pinstripe uniform for a prison uniform, spending 11 months inside for breaking various court orders. I had cancer twice and it cost me a kidney. My first two marriages were broken and my children were estranged.

In my heyday for the Mets, people put up a banner in Shea Stadium calling it "Strawberry's Field Forever." That made me laugh, but years later I remembered a line from that very Beatles song which perfectly described my life back then: "Living is easy with eyes closed." I could not see because my eyes were closed. Like the ultimate New Yorker Frank Sinatra sang, "I did it my way." But my way was destroying my life.

And so finally, after years of battling addictions, jail time, alcoholism, emotional wounds, divorces, separation from children, unforgiveness, and bitterness, I finally surrendered to God. The old baseball player, drug addict, and womanizer in me had to die. And when he did, then Jesus Christ came to live inside of me. I had my own miracle in Manhattan.

Living in freedom requires a long-term commitment to the process of change, which my incredible wife, Tracy, and I have done together. She has faithfully walked beside me and led me to a real relationship with Jesus. Our relationship with our children has now been restored. And though I used to seek solace in the crack house, we now help others recover from all sorts of addictions and substance abuse. My purpose is no longer in hitting a baseball, but in seeing others get freed forever, from what has plagued them.

As New York and the world emerge from a pandemic that has upended normality and cost many lives, a miracle story could not be more timely or hopeful. What you hold in your hands is not just one person's experience, but a collection of more than 45 real-life stories from men and women like me. We came to New York with gigantic dreams.

Whatever success we found in business, government, entertainment, medicine, or sports could not give us true significance, or save us from ourselves. But then God burst into our lives and changed everything.

Along with all of the New Yorkers who tell their stories on these pages, I was once very lost and tormented, but now I am found and free in Christ Jesus. Being a part of Every Nation Church, NYC, gave me a front row seat to watch *Miracles in Manhattan* unfold. May your life experience the same transformation!

Darryl Eugene Strawberry
September 11, 2021

INTRODUCTION

Where were you on 9/11?

It's a day permanently seared in the minds of Americans along with millions around the world. A day in 2001, when planes crashed into buildings, towers fell, and thousands died. For many, the memories of that day remain vivid. Most of us know where we were and what we were doing when Lower Manhattan took center stage. Out of the rubble of those tragic events, light began to shine in the darkness. Hope emerged, rebuilding began, and lives were changed one story at a time.

This book captures some of these stories of transformed hearts, minds, and destinies. We call these stories "*Miracles in Manhattan*," believing that a transformed life IS a miracle.

Each person featured on these pages represents countless others who, in similar ways, intersected through Morning Star New York, now called Every Nation Church, New York City, over these last 20 years. These are those who were changed and experienced renewal, some more dramatically than others, but all through the power of faith in God.

With hundreds of stories to choose from, we chose those whom we know personally and whose story we know to be true. Their faith became transformational in ways these individuals call "miraculous."

Webster's dictionary defines a miracle as "an extraordinary event manifesting divine intervention in human affairs." The stories on these pages may reflect this, or perhaps C.S. Lewis' definition when he explained, "*...a miracle is something unique that breaks a pattern so expected and established, we hardly consider the possibility that it could be broken.*" All reflect God's providence & care.

Reading stories like these makes us grateful for so many who, like those firemen and police officers running into the burning buildings on 9/11, have tirelessly served the hurting, broken and desperate. Their names may not be mentioned in these stories, but their investments cannot be forgotten.

In honor of these "essential workers," a city that rebounded, and a nation forever changed, we offer *Miracles in Manhattan,* real life accounts of tenacity, faith, and love. It's a love that believes all things, hopes all things, endures all things—a love that never fails.

Ron and Lynette Lewis
New York City
September 11, 2021

HOW IT ALL BEGAN

Ron Lewis

I can still see the smoke billowing up from Ground Zero, permanently etched into my mind.... and I still tremble.

My lifetime friend, Rice Broocks, had called me to join him two days after 9/11, for a somber drive *into* the City, while countless others were leaving. We felt compelled to do something to help, having no idea what that would mean.

Nearing the George Washington Bridge, I looked south at the rising smoke and heard these words from within, "*Out of these ashes, I will build a great church.*" I strongly sensed it was the Lord's voice and welcomed what I assumed was His heart to rebuild the church at large in New York. What I did not know then but would discover in the days and weeks to come, was my own unplanned role in this rebuilding.

While Rice and I prayed and walked the streets of Manhattan, we felt a stirring to invest. We weren't sure what that exactly meant, until an NBC news producer looked in our eyes and said, "This city is hurting and needs more churches." We had started numerous churches over the years, but never like this — without a team, a plan, a place, or start-up money. Even so, miraculous provisions began to unfold.

When Rice returned to Nashville, he stood up on the Sunday after 9/11 at his church, Bethel World Outreach, and said, "I don't know how we are going to do this, but Ron and I feel we must start a congregation in Manhattan."

Lynn Keesecker, who was visiting Bethel for the first time, approached Rice after and said, "I'm affiliated with a theater just off Times Square. You can use it."

Within six weeks, Rice and I, along with Tim Johnson, would conduct our home church services in the morning, and fly up in the afternoons to meet on Sunday nights at the historic Lambs Theater. Several others felt the call to join us, moving their families and lives into the fabric of a wounded New York City.

Out of the ashes of 9/11, Morning Star New York, later renamed Every Nation Church, NYC, began.

Frankly, the timing for my personal involvement seemed odd and misplaced. I was going through my own 9/11 as my marriage of 18 years was ending, and my four young sons were suffering. Losses on so many levels had me wondering if my work as a pastor was coming to a suffering, hopeless end.

Internal voices of doubt and condemnation rang in my ears while boarding those planes in Raleigh-Durham on Sunday afternoons. "No one in NYC wants to listen to you, a divorced minister from the south," was a droning, constant refrain.

Struggling with my own shame, insecurities, and losses, yet having a growing faith that God was working miracles on my behalf and for others, I resisted those voices and kept on trusting that God can use the "foolish things of this world to confound the wise." (I Corinthians 1:26-28).

I felt broken, but was more moved by the brokenness I saw in those faces on Sunday nights—broken hearts, shattered lives, hurting souls, abused, addicted, lustful and lonely. Very few *looked* defeated. They were young, successful, hip and beautiful. These were the young dreamers; those who knew the art of hiding shame and pain.

As Rice and I strategized on how to get the word out about our new church, we opted to try something neither of us had done before and haven't since. We raised money to run a full-page ad in a national magazine. The ad ran for three consecutive months. The unusual circumstances of a post-9/11 NYC seemed to warrant this unusual and expensive strategy. Yet to my surprise and frustration, only ONE person came from the ad. Only one, from all that time and money invested. I was frustrated and wishing I could get my money back, until I met that one person. She was a bubbly corporate professional who said, when I asked how she'd found the church, "I saw it in a magazine."

Over the next two years, that ONE turned out to be MY one—Lynette Troyer, sent by God to work in New York City, then to the church, then into my life and heart as my beloved wife, stepmom to our four sons, then mom to our miracle twin girls. All that was so broken and lost was turning around, not only in my life, but also for thousands of New Yorkers finding faith instead of fear, light instead of darkness, out of the ashes of 9/11.

Doing life with Lynette and leading this church together since our marriage in 2004 has required vision, perseverance, and the unwavering devotion of our team of pastors and leaders. In a turbulent yet extraordinary city, it has been our privilege to walk alongside so many coming out of darkness into light, out of hopelessness into purpose and meaning.

Miracles in Manhattan represents a handful of stories, which, like my own, tell of the transforming power of God, always at work even in chaos, in the backdrop of a city that keeps shining through every trial and storm.

The city is like poetry: it compresses all life, all races and breeds, into a small island and adds music and the accompaniment of infernal engines. The island of Manhattan is without any doubt the greatest human concentrate on earth, the poem whose magic is comprehensible to millions of permanent residents but whose full meaning will always remain elusive.

E.B. White, *Here is New York*

From the editors:

There are many ways a book like this can be organized. The editors have chosen to align these stories with the professional background of each person featured, even though many of these individuals cross categories in their experience and industry focus. Along with their name, a place where their miracle started or occurred is mentioned. Their bios at the end of each story share further details of who they are and what they do, highlighting the vast mosaic of New York City.

FINANCE AND WALL STREET

"Every dream has a price."
From the movie, *Wall Street.*

The New York Stock Exchange, with an equity market capitalization of $24.4 trillion dollars, is the largest of its kind. New York is a city with a bustling financial technology scene and more than 600 investment banks. The world of finance has always named it as its center.

IN MY OWN WORDS

John Luppo

East 65th Street, Midtown

I really hope you hear these words in my Italian-Bronx accent: If the Lord can do it for me, He can do it for you! I've been spared, restored, and transformed. This wasn't always my story, however. I was an alcoholic, a drug addict, a womanizer, a gambler and more.

Perhaps you've already deduced from my surname, I'm Italian-American like the other 2.6 million of us who live in the greater Metro New York area.

I was raised in the Bronx, and if you've ever seen the movies *GoodFellas* or *A Bronx Tale* featuring neighborhoods with a certain Mafia influence, that's where I grew up. I always looked up to those self-made guys with the nice cars, nice clothes, and nice-looking women. As a young man, I found it inspiring and decided it was exactly what I wanted.

In retrospect, these empty aspirations were expressing my many insecurities brought on by a negative home life. My father was an alcoholic, my brother a drug addict. My mother, a sweet Italian lady, had her own battles with codependency.

I struggled socially and wrestled with more than a handful of demons. One reason was my height. Though I felt like 6'2 because I was brash and able to fight, in reality I was 5'4 and short on self-esteem. Deep down I knew something was off, but couldn't put my finger on it. I now know much of the turmoil in my heart stemmed from my brother, Robert, overdosing at least six times. He was always in and out of addiction facilities, trying to get help but coming up empty.

I was 14 when I began drinking, starting with blackberry brandy, which I considered the best thing since sliced bread. Drinking made me talk to girls and helped me win fights. It helped me feel tall and capable, along with dark things that also came with it.

I was 18, working on Wall Street, when Robert finally succumbed to addiction and died from an overdose. My heart broke in two. I felt numb and eventually went to therapy. I also took a lot of medication and wound up in rehab for a while. After two years of sobriety, around the age of 21, I started drinking again with the same friends at the same places while ironically experiencing major success in my professional life. I had five houses, millions of dollars, and multiple girlfriends. From the outside it looked like I had it all. On the inside I had nothing.

I was nearly 40 years old when my bodyguard and driver, Anthony, gave me an Alcoholics Anonymous booklet. He had known my brother and knew I was also out of control. This good friend told me I deserved a better life.

Through attending AA meetings, I was soon sober again. My sponsor introduced me to a guy named Pati who became my best friend. His mom, Lucille, was like a second mother to me.

One Sunday, Pati wasn't answering calls, so we were forced to break down his apartment door to check on him. Tragically, we found him dead. Drugs and alcohol were the cause. The overwhelming pain took me back to when my brother had died. Once again, I was devastated.

In 2008, in memory of Robert and Pati, I produced a movie called *Modern Day Miracles* (titled *Freedom From Addiction* on Amazon Prime). During the production process, I met one of my heroes, legendary athlete

Darryl Strawberry. Darryl played for the Yankees and the Mets and was an eight-time All-Star and four-time World Series champion. It wasn't the last time we would meet.

My life on the outside looked great again with my business making over $50 million annually. My partners and I were high rollers so I rarely paid attention to the nagging emptiness I still felt inside, until one day in Miami after watching the Super Bowl, I was blindsided by depression and thoughts of suicide. My heart was hollow—I couldn't have been more distant from God.

Then I saw Darryl Strawberry again at a dinner party, and this time our conversation turned serious. He told me about Jesus and the blood that He shed for all of us, making him the first person ever to tell me what Jesus had accomplished for us on the cross. So that evening I turned my life over to Jesus completely. From that moment, I was supernaturally changed.

Fortunately, Darryl's evangelizing knew no bounds. He also introduced me to Christine, whom I married a year later. I had a new life and a new beautiful wife who is a true woman of God! We attended Every Nation Church, NYC, where I deepened my walk with God as a regular attender, and was baptized on May 20, 2012. It was a beautiful moment, but sadly there were more struggles ahead.

Serving Jesus doesn't mean everything will go our way. There are times when it can still feel impossible to get through even one more day. I had no idea the valleys I would still walk through, losing my business and many other things through circumstances beyond my control.

Through every agony and valley, through every high and low, I have learned that we all need Jesus, and we all need each other. My faith-filled friends have helped me get through these valleys. Eventually, my business came back. All that was stolen from me was restored.

God put me back on Wall Street, and I started a Bible study with my pastors, leading countless other lost souls to the only Truth that could set them free. Pastor Ron, Pastor Adam and I even launched a Bible study on a Park Avenue trading floor, which started each Tuesday, right after the closing bell.

In my own personal time of ministry with people, I have seen hundreds from all walks of life—billionaires, cab drivers, homeless people—weep and cry. Recently one of the most well-known hedge fund managers in the world asked me to pray for her.

No matter who a person is or what they do, no one can be fulfilled by this world alone. We can only be fulfilled through the saving grace of Jesus and His power to overcome. Despite a wretched past, God found me and changed me. I'll never quit thanking Him for setting me free.

Like I said before, I hope you hear this in my Italian-Bronx accent: If the Lord can do it for me, He can do it for you!

John Luppo was raised in the borough of the Bronx. He has spent years as a successful executive on Wall Street and serves his friend, Darryl Strawberry, as his ministry manager, frequently traveling with him. John and his wife, Christine, have a beautiful family and maintain a great outlook on life by helping others.

LYNETTE LEWIS

World Financial Center,
Lower Manhattan

Lynette Lewis should've been in the middle of the whole thing.

On the morning of September 11, 2001, rather than walk through the concourse of the World Trade Center as usual on her way to work, she instead got in a car service at 5:30 a.m., en route to Hartford, Connecticut. She was heading there for a marketing meeting for her firm, Deloitte & Touche, one of the "Big Four" accounting and consulting firms.

Lynette had tried numerous times to reserve a space for this meeting, not in Hartford, but at the World Financial Center where these marketing sessions were typically held. This would be the only time in her eight years of leading meetings like these for Deloitte that there would be no room in that location to hold a meeting.

Up to the last moments the morning of September 11, Lynette almost did not go to Hartford. She was fighting a serious case of laryngitis and wondered how she could possibly lead a large marketing session with no voice. Nonetheless, she hopped in the car service for the nearly three-hour drive.

Lynette and the Deloitte team were engaged in marketing discussions around 8:45 a.m., when the man next to her got a cell phone call. She heard him mumble under his breath, "A plane just hit the World Trade Center." She thought it was probably a small commuter plane that somehow veered off course. Moments later as more phones were ringing, everyone rushed down the hall to watch the TV in a small conference room.

Along with the rest of the world they sat there stunned, shocked, no one saying a word. "I'll never forget what it was like sitting in that room watching the towers fall knowing some of my colleagues in the room had loved ones inside those buildings," Lynette recalls.

Everyone dispersed and suddenly the office felt eerily empty. "I had nothing but the clothes on my back, literally, since I was not planning to spend the night," Lynette explains. Since all transportation in and out of New York City was shut down, she walked to an adjoining T.J. Maxx to buy flip flops, a t-shirt, and shorts. She checked into a hotel and sat in front of the television for the next 15 hours.

"I kept thinking how only by God's grace I wasn't in downtown Manhattan earlier that day," she remembers. "So many were tragically caught in the chaos, yet God had sent me out of town far out of harm's way that morning."

Lynette took a train back home to Manhattan the next morning. While it seemed so many others were leaving the city in droves, she had no idea a group of men from Nashville and Raleigh were heading *into* the city, one of whom would be part of her long-awaited miracle. She would later learn that this man was looking at the smoke coming up from Ground Zero as he crossed the Hudson River thinking, "That's my life right now." His marriage of 18 years was in serious trouble, and his children were in so much pain.

A few months later while in Tulsa, Oklahoma for Christmas, Lynette and her mom were looking at magazines when she came across a full-page ad titled, *Miracle on 44th Street*. The photos of Rice Broocks, Tim Johnson, Kevin Singleton, and Ron Lewis seemed to jump off the page and draw her in as she read about this new church that started because of 9/11. Her next Sunday back in town, Lynette ventured alone into the Lamb's Theatre to see what it was all about, and was deeply moved by how many visitors had driven in from as far away as D.C., Philadelphia and Boston. "I kept going back week after week, and before long knew, 'This is it—the church I've been looking for since arriving in Manhattan,'" Lynette says.

Over the next two years she dove in and served her new church. One of the pastors asked if she would help lead the growing women's ministry, which she did as a volunteer while working her 50-hour-a-week job at Deloitte. Before long this pastor, Ron Lewis, and Lynette concluded God was leading their friendship into something more.

On a chilly December evening in a church on Park Avenue, Lynette's long-awaited dream for marriage and family came true. "At 42, I married the man of my dreams *and* received four stepsons on the same beautiful night," Lynette says with a light in her eyes. "Now that's a 'more-than-enough' miracle worth waiting for!"

Over the 20 years since 9/11, Ron and Lynette have blended a family, endured years of infertility and loss, and the heartbreak of losing their son, Jordan, to cancer at age 23. "Every step of our journey we have leaned into our church family and leaders," Lynette recalls with gratitude. "We have wept together, celebrated together, launched a child-trafficking movement together, and watched multiple hundreds of lives turn from darkness to light because of the Gospel."

Lynette's gift of marriage and family turned into yet another miracle. She and Ron adopted newborn twin daughters who were born on Christmas morning, just three months before their son, Jordan, died. "God's miracles have so often seemed different than what I thought, yet better than what I imagined," says Lynette. "I will never doubt that He orders our every step. We may not understand His timing or why pain and suffering are so often part of the story, but if we keep walking and believing, miracles *will* come."

Lynette Lewis is an author, TEDx speaker, and corporate consultant. With more than 30 years' experience, she is often quoted on career development, marketing and branding. She travels extensively speaking to corporations, churches, and non-profits, has served on numerous boards, and most loves her roles of wife, mom, and grandmom.

CHRIS POTTER

Van Cortlandt Park, the Bronx

Chris Potter worked out of a gritty storefront office in Queens, selling boiler room equipment throughout the five boroughs. He wasn't a great salesman, so in an effort to discover some sense of calling, he worked hard and managed to get into Columbia Business School in 1994.

MBA in hand, two years later he went to work at an investment fund run by Lewis Lehrman, the legendary investor, who became a remarkable mentor and leader for Chris.

While at college, Chris's girlfriend had become a born-again Christian. He was attracted to what she had found: an antidote for guilt paired with the assurance of salvation. However, with no one to explain the gospel of grace to him, his interpretation of Christianity was all about "the rules," leading to three years of religious legalism void of any personal relationship with God.

"The rigidity was intolerable," Chris recalls. He started drinking when he was 23, and as his business career advanced, so did his alcoholism. Chris drank himself unconscious almost every night.

By 2001, his life was spinning out of control. His dad was diagnosed with terminal cancer. "I remember gulping a pint of vodka at 7 a.m. one morning before work, wanting only to numb the outside world," Chris recalls. "A week later I checked myself into rehab." After returning home, he had two sober months with his father before he died.

The following September, the World Trade Center towers came down. This multiplied Chris' anxiety, making the world seem more fragile than ever.

Using the turmoil of this season as a jumping-off point, he started a hedge fund—which he still manages to this day—and also began running competitively. "I'm convinced that competitive running was something God gifted me to replace drinking, whether I was open to Him or not," he says. For the next nine years, he did nothing but run and work, keeping God at arm's length.

One September evening, Chris was running on a cross-country course in the Bronx after dark. Without warning, he tripped over a bundle of tree roots, cork-screwing his right femur out of its socket and causing a fall so severe it shattered his pelvis. In agony on the ground, unable to walk and all alone in the black of night, he needed a hospital. "To get back to my car, I had to cross a narrow 200-foot bridge over a swamp," he describes. "Along the bridge I found posts to rest on after hopping on one leg. Three hops, rest on a post; three more hops, rest on a post...it was excruciating, and seemed to take forever."

Eventually, Chris made it to his car and drove to the hospital where he had eight hours of surgery and an 11-day stay. Months later, he returned to that bridge over the swamp. "Immediately, I was awed to discover that while there were posts at the beginning and the end of the bridge, there were none along its expanse as there had been the night of the accident. The way the bridge was built, there's no way they had been removed.

"25 years in the investment business has taught me to make conclusions based on data," he says. "I was clearheaded that night, high on adrenaline, and am confident of what I saw and touched. So my conclusion? I'm certain it was God who provided a way for me to get home."

While Chris was in the hospital, his mentor and former boss, Lewis Lehrman, stopped by. Lew sat at the foot of Chris's bed and said, "Everything is going to change for you now." He was right. Things had already started to change.

After years of running from God, Chris had started attending church and found God's grace. He was learning to use the gifts God had given him for a mission that mattered. "I needed my life to be more about Jesus and less about me," Chris says.

He had also started a private foundation called "All The Little Ones," loosely tied to his investment business. The name originates from the gospel of Matthew: "Take heed that you despise not one of these little ones, for I say to you, that in heaven their angels do always behold the face of my Father which is in heaven." It occurred to Chris that, "If God assigns these angels to protect the innocent little ones, then maybe I should also start there."

The foundation has brought deep meaning to Chris, enabling him to support organizations helping victims of human trafficking. These organizations include YouCanFreeUs, founded by Sujo John, one of the few people to be pulled alive from the rubble of the North Tower on 9/11.

According to Chris, so much of his journey has felt rudderless. "But in reality, God met me at every crooked bend in the road, no matter how far off course I veered. I am forever grateful and humbled by His unconditional grace and guidance. I can't imagine where I would be without Him."

Chris Potter is the principal of Northern Border Investments, a New York-based hedge fund. He is the founder of All The Little Ones Foundation and serves on the board of YouCanFreeUs. He received his MBA from Columbia University Business School. He is an avid runner and enjoys helping others find a path to financial security.

EMILIO DISANLUCIANO

Financial District, Lower Manhattan

"I was the first DiSanluciano to attend college with a full academic scholarship," Emilio DiSanluciano recounts with a combination of humility and pride. Born in Brooklyn, New York to Italian immigrant parents, he was raised in the formal traditions of their Catholic faith. He attended a Catholic grammar school and an all-boys, Jesuit high school. With an MBA in accounting and finance, he was eager to take the financial world of Manhattan by storm.

"Storms" are a fitting word for what would eventually unfold for this tall, dark, handsome Italian. By this time he had drifted from the church and principles he grew up with, ready for a rise to the top, never looking back.

Now he looks back and sees exactly what it cost him, a price he couldn't recognize at the time. "Those years of my career were all about me," he remembers. "Chasing a dollar, living in a penthouse on Wall Street, driving a Maserati, meeting women I treated like dirt. All I cared about at the end of the day was myself. I was out of control and, at times, felt out of my mind."

In addition to his self-created chaos and relentless pursuit of money, Emilio began a pattern of trusting business partners who, as he tells it, "I had no business trusting them. I took them at their word and they turned out to be bad people. Blinded by my ambition, I allowed them to drag me along for the ride."

What a ride it was. Emilio was left holding the bag for his partners' poor decisions and dishonesty, then embroiled in years of fighting to save his business and reputation. "It's a terrible thing when you do nothing wrong but are guilty by association with the company you keep," he says.

At his rock-bottom, Emilio faced an investigation that could have ended his career. It was his word against the word of others. With no idea how to survive what was stacked against him, all he could do was pray.

Up to this point he had no idea how to genuinely open up through prayer or have a sincere relationship with God. Disillusioned at a young age by what he saw as empty traditions of religiosity, the saints he prayed to seemed distant and shrouded in silence.

"I had grown tired of church rituals such as: stand, kneel, make the sign of the cross, dip your fingers in water, light a candle to a saint," Emilio remembers. "Though I respected the Catholic traditions of my family, none of it held much meaning for me. Until now—now I *had* to pray."

In the midst of this traumatizing season, Emilio had met a woman he was deeply drawn to, named Tricia. "She was different from the others." he says. "Beautiful, sincere, trustworthy. I confided in her and let her in on everything. She could tell I had lots of shame, but didn't judge me. She knew it all and stayed with me—at the lowest, most humbling time in my life."

Seemingly out of nowhere, in a revelation he can only attribute to God hearing his cries for help, Emilio was led to review a subset of emails showing communications he had with his company's lawyers. It became *the* irrefutable, factual evidence that completely shifted the entire case. Emilio was exonerated and the investigation was closed.

"I was driven to personal bankruptcy, but God brought me a miracle deliverance," Emilio marvels. "He walked me through it and out of it with my reputation intact and a chance to rebuild something new on a completely different foundation." That foundation would include his marriage to Tricia and finding a church they both love. The church baptized Emilio and Tricia, and they found an active community of friendships, constant support, and encouragement there, even through the COVID-19 pandemic.

Emilio is still amazed when he recounts the details of his journey. He thinks of others he knows who are facing trials and suffering of their own. "There are times when all we see is a crisis, but God is working out every single detail. What looks terrible for us is part of how He is digging us out of our own mess. We use terms like, 'It's hopeless; too complicated; I've messed up too much.' We're fearing the very worst. But it's not the end. I know this to be true because God made the absolutely *im*possible *possible* for me."

"I am still learning, still making mistakes," Emilio says, "But He always brings help when we call on His name. There is no way I would have ever thought about that last set of emails, but God knew. He brought me a miracle *and* redemption. Every day I live in the confidence I am forgiven, redeemed, and free!"

Emilio DiSanluciano graduated from Pace University with a combined BBA/MBA in public accounting and finance. He is a venture capitalist and an investment banker in New York City. He is most passionate about his lovely wife, Tricia, and their son, Lorenzo.

GERARD PICCO

St Bart's Café, Park Avenue

On a Wednesday afternoon at St. Bart's outdoor restaurant on Park Avenue, international realtor Gerard Picco sat with Ron Lewis and recounted his "junked-up life story," lacing his narrative with dozens of f-bombs.

Ron listened intently and responded with a simple question, the straightforwardness of which earned the businessman's respect. "Gerard, do you have a Bible?"

Consistent with the way he conversed at that time, Gerard's answer was, "Are you ****ing kidding me?" Although he was raised Catholic, reciting more than a few "Our Father's" and "Hail Mary's" in his day, Gerard was "highly skeptical of 'Christian conversion.' I was thinking of all the 'thee's' and 'thou's,'" Gerard says. "Then I recognized my hypocrisy—I was criticizing the Bible without ever having read it."

After Gerard had given his profane response, Ron, a pastor at Every Nation Church, NYC, looked him in the eye and said, "The word of God will speak to you, and if you want me to work with you, I will."

This was another response entirely new to Gerard, and it won him over. "He didn't ask me to go to church. He didn't ask me for money. He pointed me to God," Gerard recalls. So he took the advice and bought a leatherbound Bible. He also received a copy of *The Purple Book*, a biblical foundation's resource for growing in faith.

For the next several weeks he resisted opening either book.

The connection between Gerard and Ron had an interesting beginning. They met through Jim Mathers whom Gerard had met a few weeks earlier at a church service out in the Hamptons. He attended the service only because a woman he wanted to date invited him.

"I agreed to sit through that service for all the wrong reasons," Gerard remembers. He also remembers rolling his eyes at the questions presented rhetorically throughout the sermon, questions like: *Where is God in your life? What does God look like to you? What does God say to you?*

"I sat there," Gerard recalls, "and all I could say in response to the sermon was, 'God, where are You? Where are *You*?'" Then, seemingly out of nowhere something unexpected happened. He began to weep and could not stop. After the service, Gerard talked to Jim and told him he was from New York. Jim responded that he wanted him to meet somebody. That "somebody" was Ron Lewis.

"Weeks after the initial meeting with Ron at St. Bart's cafe, I was sitting alone in my bunk on my boat when I leafed through *The Purple Book* and noticed it had 12 chapters, just like my recovery had 12 steps," Gerard remembers. He was on an 11-year recovery journey from alcoholism, thanks in part to the respected 12-step program of *Alcoholics Anonymous*. This numerical parallel stood out to him and he decided to delve in, opening the Bible to Genesis.

He started reading the early verses of Genesis 3 in which Adam and Eve committed humanity's first sin of rebelling against God. Angrily, he put the Bible down. "Not this **** story! This is not going to go anywhere," he thought.

He pressed through and continued to read:

"Then the man and his wife heard the sound of the Lord God as He was walking in the garden in the cool of the day, and they hid from the Lord God among the trees of the garden. But the Lord God called to the man, "Where are you?"

"Those words, 'Where are you?' leapt off the page and transported me back to the church service when I had asked God that same question: *Where are You?* Now I was weeping once again," recalls Gerard. "It felt like God heard me and knew me. In fact, *He* was looking for *me*. For the first time, after a lifetime of nonbelief, skepticism, and hedonism, Gerard believed.

He and Ron continued meeting regularly, and Gerard connected with the church community. He read his Bible and reflected on the Word. He watched as others were making commitments to follow Christ. In just a few weeks, he was ready. Gerard loudly declared, "Jesus, I want to know you! Come into my heart, and be my Lord and Savior."

"As soon as I made that simple request, I felt something that no career, no amount of alcohol, and no relationship had ever given me," Gerard explains. "Like never before, I experienced peace. I tangibly felt the love of God fill my heart."

That was nearly 20 years ago, and Gerard still walks in the abiding peace that captured him years ago. He says with a smile and strong conviction, "The greatest privilege I have is sharing my story every day with someone who is lost and hurting like I was. It may be at the deli, on the job, in an Uber, or in the recovery programs where the same darkness that haunted my life is haunting others. I simply tell them what I found to be true: God is looking for you. He is the only one with answers for your deepest questions and pain."

Gerard often thinks back to his first snarky response to Ron's email invitation to meet him at St. Bart's:

> "Dear Ron, I don't see God, I don't know God, but, I'll agree to meet with you at St. Bart's café.
>
> P.S. Bring God with you."
>
> Ron replied by saying that he looked forward to meeting him, adding,
>
> "P.S. Don't worry, God's coming."

Gerard Picco is a native New Yorker. He's a devoted husband and father of three, and a commercial real estate consultant and contractor. Gerard brings a message of God's love and hope to everyone he meets, especially when leading a drug and alcohol-recovery ministry in the Hamptons.

DON CHOI

Olive Garden Restaurant, Times Square

Don Choi, son of Korean immigrants, grew up in northern New Jersey. He learned how to work hard and apply his intelligence to technology, math, and people. Entering the world of Manhattan as a financial and analytics professional, he took pride in being a critical thinker. Committed to studying things more objectively than most, he valued calling out injustice, inequities, and hypocrisy.

When it came to his family, Don learned "church life" was a family value and tradition, not an option. It also felt quite legalistic. Social gatherings at church were part of their regular family routine.

"Although the pursuit of God was a value to us," Don says, "it wasn't long before I saw through it. There was rampant hypocrisy with so many. Young people were calling themselves Christians around the church, then partying at clubs through the night." Troubled by what he perceived as contradictions, Don was losing all hope in the church, "I knew and even enjoyed the people but never took their faith seriously," he admits. "I just never imagined there was any power to change anyone."

Don had a friend, Hoek, from his high school, who he enjoyed spending time with and respected. Their friendship centered around a mutual love of basketball, but there was also something more. Hoek was the only person Don knew who claimed to be a Christian and really was. Don felt disappointed when they lost touch after high school.

Graduation from business school had prepared him to enter the finance world and make good money, but he also perceived a lingering, deeper issue. He describes it: "I was purposeless, directionless, and couldn't shake a low-grade depression that nagged at me day in and day out."

The depression turned him to partying and drinking. "Even while I was drunk, I still prayed," Don remembers. "I kept asking, 'God please show Yourself', yet all I was left with were doubts and skepticism."

Against all odds, on a typical summer day, Don walked into a Barnes & Noble in New Jersey and bumped into none other than Hoek. He was stunned to see the one guy he thought about so often. He wasted no time scheduling a lunch appointment.

During that lunch, Hoek asked him some basic questions, but Don skipped the pleasantries and went right to "vomiting up my feelings," as he puts it. "I don't know if I was desperate or if I just craved honesty," Don says, "but I trusted him and had a lot of respect for him." Unbeknownst to Don, prior to their meeting, Hoek was praying for him, sensing a crucial turning point was near.

Their first meeting led to a second dinner at the Olive Garden in Times Square, where they were discussing the first chapter of a book Hoek had suggested they read together. The book was titled *One2One, and it's first chapter focused* on "salvation". This discussion brought Don to a crucial decision—he was ready to receive Jesus as Lord of his life.

Hoek and Don prayed together, and God seemed near. Don hoped it would make a difference, but he wasn't sure. The next morning he was shocked to feel that something had changed. "It was like a heavy burden was lifted off of me," he recalls.

Because of this experience, he had a desire to attend church, so he joined Hoek at Every Nation Church, NYC. "I decided to lay aside former experiences, since my hunger for God was now stronger than my former disdain for hypocrites," Don says with a smile. "For the first time, it all felt real."

As he was spending time with God and feeling love, forgiveness and grace for the first time, Don's thoughts turned toward his family. Mi-Guong, his younger sister, was experiencing a form of sleep deficiency, where she would be wide awake but could not move her body at all. She told Don about "a bad spirit creeping on her," bringing night chills and sweat from the gripping fear.

Don longed to see his sister experience healing in her body and her soul, so took a chance and invited her to Israel for a tour sponsored by his church. To his surprise she said yes and invited her best friend, Tina, to come too.

Being among many of Don's new friends from the church while in Israel, made a profound impact on Mi-Guong. She found their love and sincere care irresistible to her heart. On their last night of their tour, one of the leaders, Jim Laffoon, was praying for Don when, in uncharacteristic fashion, Don started sobbing. He looked over and saw his sister and Tina kneeling and sobbing too. The experience of hearing such a heartfelt prayer for her brother led Mi-Guong and Tina to release their fear and accept Christ. Tears of repentance became tears of joy.

The miraculous changes in both Don and Mi-Guong sparked curiosity in their parents, who eventually traded their legalistic religious traditions for authentic salvation and living faith.

Marveling at how God has without a doubt ordered each of their steps, Don is still struck by one thing: "So often we doubt that one single person can really make a lasting impact on anyone. But that is all it took for me—one authentic, real Christian who I couldn't forget about for years and thankfully had not forgotten me."

He continues, "God is so deeply personal. He knows exactly who is best to reach us. For me it was Hoek. It's like it *had* to be him when I was ready to hear. God's timing is perfect, and He will find a way to get to you!"

Don Choi has worked in finance and investments at private equity hedge funds in asset management for 16 years. He is active in his church and is currently exploring new career opportunities.

JASON WARE

Lower Manhattan

It had all come down to one moment. Two and a half years of legal proceedings, sleepless nights, hollow accusations, and multiple court trials—all of it culminating here. It was now or never.

Born in Puerto Rico, Jason Ware grew up in Michigan and began his career in San Francisco and Washington, D.C. before finally moving to New York City. He made strides in his professional life until his former employer falsely accused him of violating a non-compete clause and stealing proprietary trade secrets.

Jason had left this employer to take a job with a competitor. A simple move to pursue greener pastures was now being met with a lawsuit, one that surprisingly had made it to the U.S. Supreme Court. The claimant against him was demanding a staggering five million dollars in damages.

Through the many hearings Jason learned to defend himself. Then another setback: His new employer—who had been providing legal support—went under, taking that support with them.

Years of defense were now on his back as he rushed from building to building in downtown Manhattan, trying to figure out how to file his final response. His backpack was filled with the paperwork required to respond to 84 separate motions against him, a mere fraction of the case files that filled his midtown apartment.

As his heart was pounding, Jason kept thinking about something God had spoken to him in prayer when all this started: *Do not settle. Do not file for bankruptcy. I will fight the fight for you and vindicate you—you just have to trust me and follow my instructions to the last step.*

The words he heard were opposite of the legal advice he'd received at the time. In fact, every last lawyer Jason consulted had advised bankruptcy as not only the best means of escape but the only means. Based on this word God had spoken, with no money, no background in law, and no support from anyone of note, Jason defended himself against a team of 18 lawyers and their deep-pocketed corporate plaintiff.

Now it was down to one final day. Time was running out. The documents Jason had with him must be submitted before 5 p.m., and if they were, he felt confident the judge would rule in his favor and close the case.

What he expected to take an hour when he arrived downtown at 9 a.m. began to take multiple hours. There were runarounds and dead ends. Court-building workers sent him to one court building and then back again to another. Time after time, no one could point him in the right direction. Now, late in the afternoon on a Friday, he started to panic as the offices began to wind down. Anxiety gave way to desperation.

Turning to the only person left in the building he hadn't spoken to, he approached the security guard. "Excuse me sir, do you know where the electronic court filing office is?" The man smiled, "I sure do, right this way."

The guard led Jason to the woman in charge of the electronic court filing desk. She was happy to speak with him but was quick to point out she'd be leaving early because the weather was good. She was looking forward to a long weekend lounging by the pool!

Even so, she began pouring over the case files. She looked up at Jason and said, "I'm going to help you. What's the deadline?" Jason answered, "5 p.m." They only had an hour left.

Jason kept watching the clock move closer and closer to 5 pm. "I trust you God," he kept repeating in his mind. "I believe what You promised."

The two exhaled a shared sigh of relief when the court employee's computer mouse clicked the "Submit" button, and the time appeared on the monitor, 4:59:30 p.m.

At the very last minute of the very last hour, based on Jason's filing, the court denied any further action against him and the case was dismissed. Jason got his miracle.

At a Unite NYC Walk for Justice and Equality recently hosted by his church, Jason was surprised that the walk concluded right at the door of the court buildings where he had rushed to file his case, two years earlier. There in front of the place his battle ended, he was inspired to talk about his traumatic ordeal. He was taking an experience that had been such a source of shame and now sharing it as a story of victory, to a crowd of hundreds.

"This kind of thing does not just happen," Jason began. "It was a David vs. Goliath moment and they expected me to give up. There's no way a young, Black-Hispanic man with no background in law had a chance against a corporate giant suing for five million dollars." The crowd stood riveted as Jason shared his winning outcome.

"All along the way, God led me. Step by step. From tracking down precedent-setting Supreme Court cases to the miraculous timing of that security guard in the end, God made a way out. He kept his word. God delivered the victory."

Jason Ware grew up in Puerto Rico and then moved to Michigan. He attended Purdue University for pilot school and ultimately found his passion in travel technology and financial technology. He works for Hopper Inc., and loves powerlifting, wrestling, traveling the world, and Jesus.

MIKE RISLEY

The Lamb's Theater, Times Square

In 2004, Mike Risley relocated back to New York City after living for years in south Florida. So far his life had been packed with all the things many men might dream of, but now he found himself back in the city he had left ten years earlier.

Earlier in his life, he had represented Team USA's wrestling team all over the world. "When I was a young man, wrestling was my life," Mike says. After his wrestling career ended, though, he felt as if his identity had been lost. He took up the next best adrenaline rush he could find—a career as a Wall Street trader in New York City.

With many of his friends already in that field, Mike dove in headfirst. The money and excitement went hand in hand with the party and club scene of the late 80's. Days turned into nights, and nights turned into weeks, until life itself became totally unmanageable. The drugs, the money, and the parties took front and center. Mike had lost his moral compass and felt completely lost. "I had become a slave to my sins," he remembers. "It was a whole decade before I came up for air."

Mike's first idea to "cure his sickness" was a geographical one. "Maybe if I could just leave New York and relocate somewhere with a warmer climate all my problems will go away," he surmised. His strategy backfired, however, when he landed in south Florida. Many of his New

York party buddies had already moved there, so things picked up right where they left off. Mike was running a hedge fund with nearly unlimited resources. Soon enough, he was hitting the strip clubs and doing drugs every day after work again. After ten years, he moved back to New York.

A friend began to call him and invite him to a Bible study at the Lamb's Theater in Times Square. Finally, after several months of persistent phone calls, Mike considered the invitation.

His heart was darkened and his burdens were heavy. Nothing was getting him where he wanted to go, so he decided to accept. Mike had grown up going to church, and because he was Catholic, he figured this Bible study could be a way "to cleanse himself on Sunday, with a one-hour Mass and a few Hail Mary's."

On his first visit he was challenged to define his spiritual journey. It didn't go over well. Mike decided to go back the next week and counterattack the leaders with good old-fashioned hubris. "I showed up with guns loaded to hunt down a bear, only to find an ex-NHL veteran, Adam Burt, leading the meeting." Thanks to Pastor Adam's disarming smile, they quickly became friends.

The following Sunday, Mike attended a service at the Lamb's Theatre where he met Ron Lewis. "I was a little skeptical of this smooth, southern pastor who had showed up in New York," jokes Mike. However, the two men immediately bonded.

"God gave these people a special grace and acceptance for me," Mike remembers. Through his new friends and their encouragement, he began to read the Bible daily and attend church as often as possible. This brought about a slow but positive change in his life.

He also accepted that he would never achieve perfection, something he had chased as an athlete his entire life. He was now on a journey with fellow believers who wouldn't let him "tap out" or demand a finish line.

"I chased medals and money, experienced the highest of highs and the lowest of lows, and now everything changed," Mike vividly remembers. "None of the changes could have happened without the friendship and leadership of fellow believers in Jesus Christ. Even Pastor Ron, who has four grown sons, still calls me his fifth son. He and many other men accepted me, challenged me, and called me to a whole new life."

Mike continues to stay connected with the people who mentored him along his journey. "I also try to give back those things I received in my darkest hour. I stay in the Word of God daily and stay connected to fellow believers. I help other young athletes. I'm grateful for my place in God's kingdom."

Mike will never forget all the times God protected him and brought people into his life to put him back on course. "My advice to those who are still searching and struggling is this: don't give up before the miracle happens. With God, there are no coincidences. Your own miracles will happen—God will show up, and you will be amazed."

Mike Risley was formerly a Greco-Roman wrestler with Team USA, a Wall Street trader, and the co-founder and CEO of Miami-based Caribbean Cigar Company. Mike is a Team Leader of the New York Athletic Club and the President of The Battleground Combat League. He also loves his hunting dogs.

PUBLIC SERVICE

"New York is not a city—it's a world."
Iman, actress and model

New York City has the largest diplomatic and consular community in the world. It's also home to America's largest school district and the nation's most ethnically diverse neighborhoods. As the first capital of the United States—George Washington took his first oath of office on the balcony of Federal Hall—NYC's history includes thousands of men and women who have dedicated their lives in service of a greater good. This rich tradition continues even today.

IN MY OWN WORDS

Tina Padua-Aquino
The United Nations

My husband Tim and I hopped in the car for the drive to Manhattan from our home at Rockland County, 34 miles outside the city. When we arrived at our destination, I looked up at the towering 39-story glass facade of the Secretariat Building. We were here to pray together about this new season of our lives. This was my new workplace, the United Nations Headquarters on First Avenue in Manhattan.

More than 30 years earlier in the Philippines, I was a second-grade student when my teacher displayed a photo of this very building. The image must have been captured from the same vantage point. "When I grow up, I'm going to work there!" I remember telling my teacher and classmates.

My family and I had moved to New York in 2007, crying and kicking all the way. In the Philippines, we had a beautiful home. Tim's business was doing well, and I was a few years shy of early retirement at one of the country's most prestigious employers, the Asian Development Bank.

My retirement package included exceptional medical benefits for me and my family. Our children, Samantha and Joshua, had their college education already paid. Moving to America didn't make any sense at this juncture, and most people we knew were questioning our decision.

There are those times in life when our heart is telling us one thing, while logic and our mind tells us another. Our move was one of those moments. Was God really leading us to leave so much for all that was still unknown? We felt certain He was.

After the approval of Tim's U.S. Immigrant petition, we had many confirmations that this was no pipe dream, but a true calling to leave home. From Scripture to dreams and even confirming words from people who knew nothing about us, we knew this was all from God.

We left our home, our aging parents, lifelong friends, a thriving business, and a church family we were deeply rooted in, to start anew in the United States. Though I had no job prospects at the UN, I couldn't let go of the hope in my heart for my next career journey. It was a painful and uncertain time confronting so many adjustments and changes, but like many who we were meeting in our new home church in NYC, we had come to New York because we sensed God's direction.

Within four months, through a friend of a friend, I had my first job at the United Nations Development Programme, as a consultant. Just four months later my boss recommended me for the position of Programme Assistant to the Under-Secretary-General of Political Affairs, one of the highest UN officials.

Those days at the UN were full of surprise gifts. I started a small group. The initial members were Filipinos but grew to include numerous nationalities, many of whom were deployed to the frontlines of conflict around the world.

The group earnestly prayed during some of the most precarious moments of our members' assignments:

- One of our courageous peacekeepers had an accident while leading a mission at Jebel Marra Mountain in Sudan's Central Darfur region—an incident that nearly paralyzed him.
- The Filipino peacekeepers' observer mission in the Golan Heights amidst abduction incidents.

- Another brave peacekeeper's three near-death encounters during attacks on UN personnel at Kunduz in Northern Afghanistan.
- Intercessory group prayers for the families of our UN staff and peacekeepers who were casualties during the Haiti earthquake crisis and Ebola pandemic in Liberia, West Africa.

Amidst all these challenges our group kept expanding. We've had many miraculous moments in the last few years...

When Kofi Annan, a much-celebrated Secretary-General of the United Nations, was appointed as Joint Special Envoy to the Syrian crisis, a personal audience with him allowed me to declare the Lord's blessing on him and pray for him.

I also had the opportunity to bless Secretary-General Ban Ki-Moon three times. On every occasion, he clasped my hands and thanked me with a big smile.

Because the weight of responsibility of UN staff and leaders is heavy, we've made it a point to pray consistently for world leaders, including the secretaries-general and UN senior officials. We've seen numerous UN staff go to different parts of the world, carrying with them the seeds of faith God gave them right at Headquarters.

It has now been 13 years since I entered the halls of the United Nations as a staff member. Tears fill my eyes as I remember myself as that young girl boldly proclaiming "I will work at the UN someday!" It was a dream that led me to work at a world body, rich in history and influence.

I had forgotten that dream for many years, but God did not. He brought it to fulfillment, against all odds and in His time. It required letting go of what was seen to experience what was yet unseen. The Bible refers to this process as the definition of faith, and faith does move mountains. It also moves people, sometimes across the ocean to their dreams of a promised place in a brand new land.

Disclaimer:
The views expressed herein are those of the author and do not necessarily reflect the views of the United Nations.

Tina Aquino is a political affairs international civil servant at the United Nations, serving leaders from around the world. In partnership with her husband, Timothy, she is also a marriage and family minister, mom to Samantha (married to Jonathan) and Joshua (married to Gabrielle), grandma to Raine, with one more grandchild on the way.

KATHY AND LUCIANO

Three Mile Harbor Road, East Hampton, NY

It was a late night drive on the beautiful Three Mile Harbor Road in the Hamptons, July 4th, 2003. The road was eerily deserted on this holiday weekend. But something in the distance caught the eyes of the two men driving.

Gerard Picco and his friend, Ron Lewis, drove closer and slowed down. They could see a car flipped over in the middle of the road with its lights still on. Its wheels were spinning like an oversized toy, the engine still running while the man inside kept screaming, "Kathy! Kathy!"

About 40 feet away, a woman was lying face down in the street. Ron ran over and knelt beside what seemed like a lifeless body. "This has to be Kathy," he thinks. Even in the dimly lit street, he could see a trail of blood running from her mangled frame. Running to the car to see if he could help the man get out, Gerard saw the man begin to climb out of the car, seemingly unhurt, so he ran over to Ron and knelt down with him over Kathy. Ron was praying intently, though Kathy showed no signs of life—no movement whatsoever. "I later learned that she was called in dead by whoever called 911, and it certainly looked that way in the moment," Gerard vividly recalls.

Now out of the car, the man was still crying, "Kathy, Kathy!" By this time several vehicles had stopped, and a crowd was gathering. The urgent wail of approaching sirens could be heard in the distance. Ron's prayers escalated from whispers to words spoken out loud with conviction.

"I had never heard anyone pray like that," Gerard remembers. New to the faith, all he remembered from his Catholic upbringing was the Lord's Prayer, which he recited over and over. He had to pray something, anything, to try and help. Ron opened his hands out wide as if to pray a last desperate prayer, then paused for a couple of seconds. He reached over and gently laid his hands on Kathy's bloody back, saying, "In the name of Jesus, Lord, give her breath. In Jesus' name, BREATHE."

At first nothing happened. Gerard looked into Ron's determined face, searching for resignation, then back again at the still body. Motionless. Nothing. Blood everywhere. Then suddenly, the dress on the woman's back began to move, up and down, ever so slightly at first. Then came a loud, raspy, wheezing gasp, next a cough, a cough that rattled with blood.

"It sounded as if a massive amount of air was being pushed through a straw," Gerard remembers. The woman turned her head just a little bit, but enough to send waves of relief through the witnesses who had gathered. After several minutes of lying motionless and crushed she was alive! Breathing! Gerard had no words for what he was seeing. He was stunned and in awe.

The paramedics arrived and took over, as Ron and Gerard gave their eyewitness report to the Hamptons police. Shaken, but rejoicing, they arrived at Gerard's home around 3:00 a.m. "I watched Ron wash his hands, washing blood off of his skin and clothes like he was sending the devil's desire for death down the drain," Gerard remembers.

The next day, Gerard called the police department to find out to which hospital Kathy had been sent, and if the man who had been with her was okay. No one would give him any information. Gerard told the whole story to the person on the phone, trying to find a lead. Finally, the very kind sergeant told Gerard, "I'm not supposed to do this, but..." and shared the name of the hospital where Kathy was admitted.

Visiting the hospital the next day with his Bible in hand was a novel experience for Gerard, a new believer. He met Kathy's parents in the hospital room where she was still unconscious. Her head was swollen, twice its original size. She had a broken hip and leg. Her parents shared the doctors expected her recovery would be partial, long, and hard because of the head injury.

"Hearing this report, I remembered one of the verses in Psalm 139," Gerard recalls. So I read it to her parents and to Kathy, despite her unconscious state. "I praise You because I am fearfully and wonderfully made; Your works are wonderful, I know that full well," Gerard read the passage with faith and sincerity. As the weeks went on, Gerard, Ron and the Every Nation Church, NYC family kept praying vigilantly for Kathy and her family.

After several weeks Gerard returned to the hospital to check on Kathy and was directed to a visitor area on the rooftop. The sun was setting as he saw the silhouettes of a man, a few children, and a lady in a wheelchair. As he approached them, the man stood up. Surprisingly, the lady in the wheelchair—Kathy—stood up too. The man, Kathy's husband Luciano, said, "You are our angel." Gerard had been called a lot of things as a New Yorker, but never an angel! Gerard told them details about that night when Ron knelt down over Kathy, praying in the name of Jesus that she would breathe and live. Tears of awe and wonder poured down each face, hearing the full story of their miracle on Three Mile Harbor Road.

Now, many years later, Kathy is fully recovered. She's been 100% healthy for a long time, teaching children, always smiling and loving everyone around her—all by the grace of God.

Kathy and Luciano are Gerard's friends and neighbors in the Hamptons. "They come with us to the Hamptons Church, where Pastor Joe and Margarette have befriended them, and every time Ron visits it's like a family reunion we never want to end," Gerard recalls with a smile. Luciano, in his strong Italian accent, never stops saying, "God sent these beautiful men, these angels that night when we experienced the love of God."

Gerard sums up one lesson he learned from that unforgettable July 4th weekend, when he watched a miracle happen right before his eyes. "Watching Ron pray like he did that night when it all looked hopeless has helped me remember that when I doubt God, I just need to be still and not give up. Because the miracle may just need five more minutes. Five minutes. That's how long it took for Kathy to start breathing again."

Kathy and Luciano live in East Hampton, New York. Luciano is a mason contractor and a business owner, and Kathy is a public school educator. They have two grown children and a very happy family.

GIOVANNY CAMPOS

The Deli on 92nd Street and Madison Avenue

Giovanny Campos had his first encounter with God at the age of 16 when he "accidentally" ended up in a church service. It turned out he really liked it. Never before had he found such peace—all his troubles seemed to vanish.

When his peers gave him a hard time for going to church, he stopped attending, but that true, pure feeling of joy and happiness remained a memory for a very long time.

15 years later he was working at a well-known restaurant in New York City, often into the early hours of the morning. Totally exhausted with his job, he prayed that God would help him find a new direction in life. A few days after that prayer, he got in a taxi at 92nd and Madison Avenue around 2:00 in the morning, and asked the cab driver to stop at a nearby deli. He hopped out wearing his suit and long black coat, looking more like a gangster than a restauranteur. Walking up to the counter in the deli, he asked for a pack of Marlboro Reds.

"You know, I quit those," said a voice coming from behind him. He turned around to see a tall, gentle-looking man waiting in line with a box of cereal. "Oh, really. How did you do it?" Giovanny asked.

"God helped me," the man said. They struck up a brief conversation and before heading their separate ways, the man handed him his card, saying, "If you ever want to quit smoking, please call me."

Giovanny went home exhausted, not thinking much more about it, until the next day when he couldn't resist calling the man from the deli.

The man's name was Gerard Picco, who shared his salvation story with Giovanny over breakfast that next day. God had completely changed Gerard's life—nicotine addiction was the least of his problems. "I can only point you to God," emphasized Gerard. "It's up to you if you want to accept Him." Gerard was quoting his pastor at Every Nation Church, NYC, who had said those very words to Gerard just a few years earlier. Giovanny was ready this time, and unlike before, he would not shrink back.

Accompanying Gerard to church a few days later, he listened to the message with attentive ears, getting the distinct feeling that Pastor Ron was talking directly to him, calling out his specific situation. He felt frozen in place but recognized that same undeniable peace he had felt back at his first church experience—a peace once again pouring over him.

After the service, Gerard introduced him to the pastors and many more, and from that night forward Giovanny became a regular attending member of Every Nation Church, NYC. "I was grateful for Gerard's intentional and sincere care for my life," recalls Giovanny, "and for the additional men and women I was meeting at the church. They had great hearts and were committed to helping me without harboring any sort of ulterior motive or selfish aim.".

"I'll never forget that night—2:00 a.m. at 92nd and Madison Avenue. The night when a man simply went out for a box of cereal and ended up saving my life. For a long time I thought it was him—Gerard—who had found me, a desperate soul wandering like a lost sheep. Now I know it was *God* who found me. There at that deli on the Upper East Side of Manhattan, God came looking for me."

Giovanny Campos has been a restaurateur and sommelier much of his adult life. Starting at the extraordinary Ryland Inn in New Jersey, and later managing fine dining locations in NYC, he launched his own restaurant, sold it, then shifted to management positions at the Palm Court Restaurant at the Plaza Hotel and more.

ADOLFO OSSO

Times Square Church

Adolfo Osso was in his mid-twenties, heartbroken, divorced, and beginning to slide into a lifestyle of hard-core partying. He went out on the town every night, throwing money away on whatever he could think of that might fill his emptiness. No matter what he tried, he could not escape the loneliness of New York City. Born in Buenos Aires, Argentina, Adolfo had graduated from high school with two job skills: electronic technician and auxiliary airplane mechanic. At 21, he moved to work at his father's small plumbing business in New York. It was a hard transition, but he accepted this occupational role.

Making a lot of money and spending even more, he felt desperate and kept grasping for anything that might give him answers. Over the course of just a few years, he paid fortune tellers more than $30,000. Eventually the grind of his self-described "empty, aimless life" left him desperate. "I needed 'change' more than anything in the world," Adolfo remembers, "but had no idea how or where to find it."

A woman who worked as hostess at the restaurant where he went regularly to drink kept inviting him to church. She also gave him something he knew little about—a Bible. He was attracted to her happy smile and joyful face, so he eventually accepted her invitation.

Showing up at a church in Times Square was an entirely new experience for Adolfo. People around him were talking in various languages, and raising their hands as the choir up front sang many songs he didn't know. The woman with whom he had come to church began weeping. Adolfo wasn't sure what any of it meant, however, he liked the girl so much he decided to raise his hands and embrace the feeling of the moment.

"All of a sudden, I felt something hot coming down from my hands, over my body, and down to my feet," Adolfo remembers. "I was struck by this tangible, undeniable feeling I'd never had before."

Over the next week he kept pondering what it all meant, so he was glad when he ran into his fortune tellers on the street. "Maybe they'll know what this seemingly spiritual experience is that just happened to me," Adolfo thought. What they said surprised him, and he later learned the irony of what they said: "That was the Holy Spirit."

Adolfo decided to visit the church again and never went back to the fortune tellers, except to pray with them and share his newfound faith. Over the course of the coming months, going to church and attending Bible studies brought a feeling of abiding peace in his soul. For the first time in his life, Adolfo had a sense of purpose and hope. "I finally found what I was looking for, and it was all by God's grace."

Not too long after, he asked Pastor Ron Lewis to pray for him to quit smoking. "I've never had a cigarette since," Adolfo marvels. So many old patterns were becoming new. His growing friendship with church leaders and new friends helped him walk away from the lifestyle he had before. His best gift? Marrying Patricia, the beautiful restaurant hostess who had first invited him to church.

"Though I spent many years living hopeless, without a dream of anything meaningful, Pastor Ron and I started dreaming together about starting a Spanish-speaking church," Adolfo remembers. The two men went to Honduras on a mission trip, where they were both impressed with the young man who was Ron's translator.

"Unlike me at his age, this man was strong and confident, with passion and talents we all noticed right away," says Adolfo. He and Ron left Honduras discussing practical ideas about helping this young leader, Joseph Ford, come to NYC. Joseph soon relocated, and now leads the Every Nation Hispanic congregation in the Bronx, where Adolfo, Patricia, and their three daughters helped this special church begin.

Adolfo is still amazed at how his days of aimless wandering, searching for so long to find peace and meaning, are now just a memory. He is the president of Osso Plumbing and Heating Corporation, and Patricia has worked at the United Nations for 15 years.

Through a persistent invitation from a woman he didn't yet know, Adolfo had experienced a miracle. He learned how to trust God with all his heart and walk in the teachings of Jesus that have power to change a life. Adolfo summarizes his journey by saying, "So often people think they have to get 'good enough' for church, and somehow be 'ready' to serve God. But the truth is He found *me* and looked beyond my sin and shame. When I was utterly lost, before I had any idea who He is or what I needed—this is what amazes me—the Good Shepherd came looking for me."

Adolfo Osso is an Argentinine, son of Italian immigrants, who moved to New York when he was 21. He is President of Osso Plumbing, a business his father started in NYC more than four decades ago. He became a father at 47, is married to Patricia Pantoja and they have 3 daughters.

ELISA ZINN

A Target store in South Jersey

Brokenhearted, shattered, embarrassed, and clueless about what to do next describes how Elisa Zinn felt at the outset of 2003. It was not how she expected the new year to begin.

She was supposed to be preparing for her wedding four weeks out, but had just broken it all off *and* quit her teaching job. Her parents had recently sold Elisa's childhood home, having resigned from the church they pastored most of her life, moving to a new state that had nothing to offer her. Elisa had no fiancé, no job, no home or refuge, no church, and no plan.

She was quietly praying and shopping aimlessly around a Target store in south Jersey when she ran into an old friend, Tina, who invited her to travel together with their mutual friend, Melissa for a drive to New York City to attend a church they had been visiting in Times Square.

"What was remarkable to me," Elisa remembers, "is that I had already heard of this church and had tucked the information card in my Bible to remind me to check it out." That Sunday night they made the more than two hour drive to Lamb's Theater where a tangible buzz of excitement was in the air. "When worship began," recalls Elisa, "I knew immediately the presence of God was among us. Then I heard the pastor say, 'When you find your people you find your purpose,' and I knew that this was home."

Tina and Elisa were both sure they wanted to be a part of this church, Every Nation Church, NYC. Wasting no time they moved from New Jersey and settled in Queens, finding an apartment and steady jobs.

Other friends back in New Jersey were now filling cars on Sunday afternoons, driving to join them at the evening services. These friends were looking for something more too, and wanted to experience this place with its inspirational testimonies of lives changed every week.

After a year of living in New York, the Lord inspired a surprising change in Elisa's heart about a move back to the south Jersey area. She thought, "My parents gave so much of their lives in south Jersey, what on earth could there possibly be for me back there?" Interestingly, Tina was also feeling the nudge to go back.

Just a few days later the senior pastor, shared news during the church service: they would be starting new church sites, saying specifically, "We will be planting in Philadelphia." Elisa, Melissa, and Tina simultaneously let out a shout, knowing South Jersey is just across the river from Philly. This news confirmed all that had been stirring in their hearts.

Elisa marveled at how the details were coming together, reflecting on this journey that began one average afternoon in Target. In little more than a year, she had moved from New Jersey to New York City, been trained, equipped, and encouraged, and now God was moving her again, to be part of launching something new in her old backyard.

"Along with several people from NYC, we started holding monthly services at the Radisson Hotel in South Jersey," Elisa remembers. "New people were finding us each month, and a few players from the Philadelphia Eagles NFL team had already come on board to help with Bible studies and prayer meetings. There was a sense of excitement and expectation."

Before long, David Estes and his wife, Kathleen, staff members of the New York church, moved to Philadelphia to pastor what was now a growing congregation. They eventually named the congregation Freedom Church Philadelphia.

In the years since then, under the leadership of Dr. Gabriel Bouch and his wife Jennifer, many hundreds have been baptized at the two Freedom Church locations: Center City, Philadelphia and Merchantville, New Jersey. Elisa's seemingly "random" outing to Target turned her disappointments into a miraculous adventure. "I even fell in love with one of the men that drove up from south Jersey each week in those early years," Elisa marvels.

That man was Paul, and together they have served in many leadership roles. Elisa was privileged to give the Sunday morning message just a few months ago. Jeremy Moore, also a part of that original group of commuting friends, is now one of their site pastors.

"Even when things look like they aren't going according to plan, *God* has a plan, and *that* plan is always better than what we can think or imagine," declares Elisa. God used the big, lonely city of New York to surround me with people of faith, heal my heart, put me back on my feet, and reveal his purpose for my life."

She summarizes by saying, "I am forever thankful for the obedience of those who followed the call of God after the World Trade Center towers fell. They came to help restore a city with the healing gospel of Jesus, and through them, God restored me."

Elisa Zinn and her husband Paul, a businessman, serve at Freedom Church NJ in various leadership roles for the worship and ministry teams. Elisa is a gifted speaker and has created an online sisterhood, SorellaLIVE. She is also a proud homeschool-mama to her three children.

CHRIS TANG

Bensonhurst, Brooklyn

Chris Tang had consumed too much alcohol at a family party and passed out while lounging in the backyard pool. It was dark outside and the pool was dimly lit. Without anyone noticing, he slipped down and slowly sank to the bottom.

Nobody knows for sure how long this lasted, but according to most who were present, Chris was completely submerged for at least five minutes—maybe longer. When he was discovered, everyone there started to pray—even if they had never prayed before—and immediately someone dialed 911, so sure that he was dying. They were shocked when the ambulance arrived only five minutes later.

As his family and friends walked into the emergency room lobby, they were traumatized. The doctors rushed him back and before long reported that Chris' lungs were nearly 75% filled with water. It seemed impossible he could survive.

Just two months earlier life had been unusually good for Chris. His business in New York City was growing, his relationships were standing strong, and most importantly, for the first time in his life, Chris felt whole in spirit, soul, and body. "To put it simply, Jesus found me," Chris explains. "I was experiencing the Holy Spirit every day, hungry for more, and desperate to know the Word of God."

In this season of spiritual renewal, Chris had started praying what would turn out to be a prophetic prayer: that the supernatural peace he had finally found would spread like fire through the rest of his family. He longed to see his loved ones experiencing the living God in their personal, day-to-day lives.

One night in his Brooklyn apartment he went so far as to pray, "Lord, whatever it takes to see my family come to You, please let it come to pass. I'm more than willing to sacrifice for them, but please don't let them suffer." Two months after that prayer, the unthinkable happened.

Now Chris lay unconscious in the hospital with his life in the balance. His family and friends kept praying for him as news of his horrible tragedy started to spread. Everyone was desperately crying out to God for his survival.

Remarkably, after two days of total unconsciousness, Chris woke up! He was alert and of a sound mind, an answer to hundreds of prayers. His quick recovery and healing were extraordinary. The medical professionals tending to his bedside were shocked. Even they used the word "miracle." For Chris, though, the real miracle was that through those waiting, anguishing days, his family had experienced God and the presence of the Holy Spirit, just as he had asked for months earlier in his apartment.

Weeks later, Chris sat down with his mother to talk about his time in a coma. She told him that when she was consumed with fear, she recalled the words Chris had shared with her prior to the accident when he told her, "We can pray and ask God to heal the sick because we have Christ within us. His power is greater than sickness or disease."

Those words had come back to her, even though she hadn't thought much about it when he said them. She prayed for a miracle and when it was fulfilled, she understood the Holy Spirit in a whole new way—a way she might not have known if not for this terrible accident. Her faith had been activated in a whole new way.

Chris's near-death experience and extraordinary recovery was a horrifying experience for many. However, it became a turning point for many as well. Reflecting back, he says, "I simply have no words anymore, except to say that miracles are real and anyone can experience them. I also know prayer works! So when you're praying for a miracle, don't quit praying!"

Chris Tang will never forget the goodness of God in his life. As he talks about his miracle he often shares with friends and strangers alike, "My relationship with God is everything."

KELLI MCDANIEL

Upper West Side Manhattan

21 years old and looking for a fresh start, Kelli McDaniel had recently graduated college *and* finished her last round of chemotherapy. "The day after my final checkup the doctor gave the 'all-clear,' so I packed my bags and drove across the country to New York City, my new home and new beginning."

As part of the New York City Teaching Fellows program, Kelli's first years were stressful and challenging. She was quickly immersed in a high-needs neighborhood in the city, with no training for the countless obstacles she would face in the education field.

Amidst long hours at work and still recovering from the post-traumatic stress of battling cancer, she started experiencing something out of the ordinary. "Interesting things I couldn't explain," she recalls. "Vivid, supernatural dreams and visions would wake me up in the middle of the night, leaving me with a deep, strange need to pray for the city." Kelli sensed the burdens of strangers as she walked down the streets of Manhattan. "I could feel their pain viscerally, prompting me to pray."

Looking for a stronger support system, she started attending Every Nation Church, NYC on Sunday nights, giving her a fresh way to know God and connect with a community committed to bringing help and healing.

"It was in that season," Kelli remembers, "that God was encouraging me that yes, I would find my own healing, but would also lead others into freedom, and one day become a school principal." She wasn't sure how it would all happen, but these dreams brought much-needed motivation and encouragement.

Against a daily backdrop of stress and long days on the job, deep emotional wounds from her past seemed to resurface. "Though I had been through years of therapy, having read every self-help book on the shelves. the severe traumas of my past still hurt and were keeping me bound up." Kelli remembers. "I was far from free."

Then her church introduced her to "Cleansing Stream", a multi-week interactive program founded by pastor Jack Hayford in Los Angeles. It became the transformational catalyst that liberated her from oppression, bondages, and even spiritual curses. Kelli finally had the tools to walk in freedom and discover sustainable joy. "I became a new person who could recognize what God had been offering me all along. I was living differently—people around me were also noticing the dramatic changes," she recalls.

Kelli finally felt whole and loved. She also felt commissioned. "One of my favorite passages in the Bible is in the book of Isaiah, chapter 61, which says that, 'The Spirit of the Lord God is upon me, because the Lord has anointed me to bring good news to the poor; He has sent me to bind up the brokenhearted, to proclaim liberty to the captives, and the opening of the prison to those who are bound; to proclaim the year of the Lord's favor.'" Kelli explains. "Though this passage is referencing Jesus, it can apply to everyone. No matter what our profession or job might be, we can help bring others into freedom."

Since that season of intense healing, Kelli has solidified her calling to bring justice and equal opportunities to the impoverished and disadvantaged. She also volunteers as the director of Cleansing Stream where along with other team members she has seen over a thousand people find freedom and healing in Christ.

Kelli arrived in New York City with a two-year plan, but is currently entering her 19th year as an educator, serving as an assistant principal at a school in the Bronx. She is also teaming up with two friends and fellow educators to work on a God-sized dream: starting a charter school called Clay Academy. "Our vision for Clay is to plant a nontraditional school in the heart of the South Bronx, within the poorest congressional district in the nation."

The South Bronx community has the highest percentage of homelessness in New York City, a tragic amount of youth in foster care, and a strong prevalence of mental illness. Kelli and her team plan to join forces with the community, flip the script, and bridge the divide in a borough plagued with trauma, poverty, and disproportionately distributed resources.

Kelli came to NYC broken and defeated, but today her passion is to offer renewal, healing and freedom to the young people of the city, equipping them to reach their highest potential. In her words, "I experienced my miracle in Manhattan through the power of God and the inner presence of His love. I'm forever grateful to serve and give all I am, so this diverse city can be transformed one life at a time."

Kelli McDaniel began her career in the NYC Department of Education in 2003. She is an assistant principal of an elementary school in the Bronx and is devoted to children and families in many capacities. Director of the Cleansing Stream Ministry at her church, Every Nation Church, NYC, she has been active in leading inner healing for over 10 years.

UNIVERSITY STUDENTS

He who opens a school door, closes a prison.
Attributed to Victor Hugo, playwright and author of **Les Misérables**

The backdrop for more than 100 colleges and universities and the nation's largest K-12 school district, New York City has an academic reach whose influence spans the globe. With more than one million college students in the city each year, campuses have not only equipped future leaders of government, science, arts and industry, but are often the places where far-reaching personal plans for the future take root, and where lifetime friendships begin.

IN MY OWN WORDS

Dr. Joseph Marlin
New York University

During my childhood in our Jewish home, I was part of a long religious tradition. I thought of my rabbi as a holy man every time I saw him, and often felt a powerful presence when we went to temple. I attended Hebrew school and, like many Jewish boys, had a bar mitzvah and prayed the Shema.—the Jewish confession of faith. But when I hit my junior year of high school, I decided to stop praying because I didn't feel like anyone was listening.

Two of the first friends I made at the University of California in Berkeley were Christians. They invited me to events and gave me books, but I wasn't interested. Another Berkeley friend from back home in Los Angeles invited me to the Campus Hillel, a Jewish cultural group. Although I went a couple of times, I never felt like I belonged or wanted to be there. Slowly my early adulthood drifted into agnosticism.

In 2008, I moved to New York City to study at New York University's combined MD and PhD program. By that time the idea had captured my mind that religion really was antiquated and that science was the future. I thought I was going to be part of the mission to make science the universal belief system and help usher in a second scientific revolution.

I became a dedicated atheist, listening to debates and reading books by famous atheist authors. As an "evangelist" for atheism, to me, science was the answer.

In the middle of all this, something life-changing happened. I started my graduate neuroscience courses and was attending a lecture one October day in 2010. I guess it was boring because I started to drift off into a daydream. Then I saw what can only be described as a divine vision.

> *I was walking along a sidewalk in a place that felt like Brooklyn on a sunny day with a beautiful blue sky. There were other people walking on the sidewalk and cars in the street, when all of a sudden the sky turned gold and was full of light. Everyone stopped and looked up. I too stopped and looked up. We waited there expectantly.*
>
> *Then a booming voice came out from the sky: "I am the Lord thy God." The cars stopped. All of us sank to our knees and wept. I was filled with an incredible sense of peace because I knew I didn't have to fight anymore.*

The vision ended abruptly and my first thought was, "That was weird!" I never had a feeling of peace like that before, and now believe I was experiencing the presence of the Holy Spirit, although I didn't know it at the time. I snapped out of it and went back to listening to the lecture. I didn't remember, think, or talk about the experience for several months.

I was dating a Christian girl, Bianca Jones, at the time. As a gag gift on Valentine's Day 2011, I bought her a pack of tarot cards. Very offended, she threw it straight into the trash and we entered into a vigorous debate about faith. That's when I remembered the vision. I described it to her, and she said, "We need to get to a church." In that moment, I began wondering in a serious way what faith meant in my life.

I found myself drawn to reading the Bible. Growing up I had been taught the names of the first five books of Moses but never actually picked up the Bible, not even Jewish scripture. When I opened Matthew 1 in the Bible I had just purchased, I read the genealogy tracing Abraham to David, and David to Jesus. These were names I remembered from Hebrew school.

"Oh I remember Abraham," I told myself, "I have heard of David and can see now, it ends with Jesus." It was a special moment for me. As a Jewish person I was experiencing Christianity in a way I had never thought of before, as a continuation of my own family's faith tradition from Abraham and now to the Messiah, Jesus. In the next few months I devoured the Bible, fascinated by the Old Testament, the New Testament, all of it! I attended a church service with Bianca, but came away offended and angry. She convinced me to try one more church and we found Every Nation Church, NYC.

The service was held on the Upper East Side. Pastor Bruce Ho captured my attention when he said, "Sometimes God offends your mind to reach your heart." I was surprised because that was exactly what had happened to me at the other church. A pathway opened into my heart in that moment, somewhere between the thing that offended me and the Lord who led me forward.

I'd never considered talking to Jesus nor considered the possibility He might be real, alive, seeing me, listening to me. In prayer, I introduced myself to Him and had a sense He talked to me and knew me. It sort of made me smile, though I felt a little silly for introducing myself to the God of the universe.

My journey with Jesus had begun. Pastor Bruce Ho met me in his apartment for breakfast to talk through the *One2One* discipleship primer. I also met Pastor Ron Lewis, who like me is from a Jewish background. We rejoiced together that we had found our Messiah.

In 2012, I was baptized at the church office on West 51st Street, and became a new person completely. Bianca and I married the next year, and both earned our PhDs in Neuroscience. She became an assistant professor at Columbia University while I finished my residency at NYU and moved into the extraordinary world of psychiatry. We are blessed with two beautiful children who we are raising to know the living God.

I'm grateful at every turn for God's presence, His grace, and for the saving work He did on the cross for me, taking me out of unbelief and struggle into love, acceptance, hope and faith.

Dr. Joseph Marlin is a psychiatrist practicing in New York City. He received his MD and PhD from NYU, where he met his neuroscientist wife, Bianca. Together they have two children who love to dance and play ukulele.

SAMANTHA PARKER

American Musical and Dramatic Academy, Lincoln Square

"God, are you there?" Samantha asked, looking up to the heavens—the ceiling of her New York City apartment bathroom. She was hopeless in a city full of promises, promises that had left her with questions and heartbreak.

Things hadn't started out that way. Samantha was in her twenties when she moved from Bristol, England, to study at the American Musical and Dramatic Academy (AMDA) on Manhattan's Upper West Side.

"I couldn't wait to have the 'Sex and the City' lifestyle," she remembers. "From a young age, I liked boys and loved to party, get drunk, smoke and show off my body. My life was a lot of fun and I was a heartbreaker for lots of men."

Her move to NYC turned out to be much harder than expected and not exactly the "Charlotte, Amanda and Carrie" dream she had envisioned. Graduating from AMDA felt like a small victory, but she wondered what struggles she would face next.

Finding herself involved with a guy that "drained the life out of her," she was several months into the very emotionally charged relationship when she became deeply depressed, losing too much weight, and most of her friends. "I was in a very dark place," Samantha remembers. "The ambition and zest for life that brought me to New York had stopped, and now I wondered if any of my habits and hobbies were worth anything anymore."

Sometimes, however, gardens can grow in the lowest, most unexpected places.

One day, her boyfriend shared some startling news—he now believed in Jesus. "My jaw nearly hit the floor," Samantha remembers. She knew the kind of lifestyle he had lived up to this point, and felt "disgusted over his ridiculous decision."

Curious nonetheless, Samantha started asking questions about Jesus. Her boyfriend was reluctant to share at first, but soon opened up, sparking an even greater interest in her unsettled mind and heart. She was learning many new things from him, like, *You can pray to God anytime, anywhere*, an incredibly eye-opening revelation for someone raised in a formal church that relegated God to Sundays only. "I had never been told that you could have a personal relationship with God, much less have it every day and anywhere," she says. "My experience of Christianity was going to a boring church and kneeling in the pews to pray. I searched for more to life for years, but never did I imagine Jesus was the one I was looking for."

It was directly after this that she talked to God in her bathroom the very first time, asking, "Do you really exist?"

About a month later, Samantha asked God why she couldn't give Him full control of her life, despite her desire to do so. "I want you to have control," she prayed, "But how do I do it?" Moments later she was experiencing a powerful, overwhelming sensation, a tangible change in her mind, body, and soul.

"Thanks to the power of God revealed in that moment, my heart underwent a miraculous transformation. I let Him in fully, ready to give Him my all," Samantha remembers. She bought her first "Beginner's Bible" the very next day.

Reading the Bible began to open her eyes to her sin. The stories brought conviction and she committed to rise above her repetitive mistakes. "I was having very personal experiences with God but still, in many ways, I was barely keeping my head above water," she recalls.

The unhealthy relationship with her boyfriend only made things worse. In the past Samantha had tried to hide the painful wounds coming to the surface from the relationship, but now she yearned for healing and wholeness, looking for freedom that would last.

One rainy New York night, Samantha cried out at the top of her lungs for help. And God responded in what to her was strong clarity, leading her to return to England to distance herself from this man and her past. "It was the first time I received distinct direction from God, and felt I had the ability to follow through," she remembers. Two weeks later, she was on a flight to London. Back home in England, Samantha saw God continue to work in surprising ways.

MySpace, a popular hub during the dawn of online social media, brought a connection with Brian Parker, a friend who had recently become a Christian. When she returned to New York City, Brian invited Samantha to attend Every Nation NYC. "With all my posts on MySpace, he noticed I was sorely lacking a faith-based community," she remembers.

Samantha found that community at church where she met two women her age who helped her understand how to walk with God every day in real, transformative ways. "The church became MY belonging SPACE, filled with life-giving friends."

It wasn't long before Brian and Samantha's relationship went from friendship to more than that, built upon a foundation with God at the center. They married, and Samantha went on to work for a non-profit the church helped to create to fight child sex-trafficking. She found her community, her husband, and now a life-giving calling, one that brought freedom and answers to others.

Samantha looks back on her early questions and realizes, "Yes, God was there all the time, listening and leading me to purpose and joy beyond my dreams."

Samantha Parker is based in Sacramento, CA, with her husband, Brian. They have three lovely children they adopted from foster care: Callum, Liam, and Malaya. The couple's adoption decision originated from Samantha's work with Lynette Lewis at StopChildTraffickingNow.

BERTINA HU

The Lamb's Theater, Times Square

Bertina Hu was just 14 years old when she lost her mother to cancer. "As a family, we were unable to process emotionally and mourn her death," she vividly recalls. "So I suppressed my confusion, grief, and anger for years, and blamed it on my dad."

When she was a junior in high school, for a school assignment she shared some journal entries she had written, describing her grief and anger. The English teacher asked her about them. "My teacher saw behind what I took as just 'emotional processing' and encouraged me to initiate an honest conversation with my dad."

"I'll never forget that day in the car with my father, the day when I felt brave enough to start talking about it," she remembers. He listened from the driver's seat, tears streaming out of his eyes, saying "I'm sorry, I'm sorry" over and over again. Their relationship changed that day, and while Bertina felt somewhat of a breakthrough, there was still much more work in her soul to be done.

"From high school into my early twenties, I believed my self-worth depended on doing good deeds and pleasing other people," she says. "So I made a vow to 'major in being a good person.'" Despite Bertina's well-intended commitment, she was often filled with fear and a general lack of purpose.

The "do good be good" aspiration led her into self-described "lustful and destructive short-term relationships," whether it was being someone's girlfriend or clubbing with her friends. "I may have given off the impression that I was confident and had it all," Bertina remembers. "But I was afraid of abandonment, failure, death, and not being good enough."

A glimmer of hope emerged when she met Michelle Choi during her first year at the all-female Bryn Mawr College in Pennsylvania. They grew close, like sisters, and in September, 2006, moved to New York City. The first Sunday there, Michelle was heading for a church service at the Lamb's Theatre and invited Bertina to join her. "I had plans to find a Catholic church but, for whatever reason, decided to go with Michelle instead," Bertina remembers.

Lynette Lewis, a corporate woman, was giving the message that evening, and Bertina was "crying buckets" throughout the service. The message was about finding purpose beyond a job description or a degree. "I felt what I can only describe as 'God's love tugging at my heart,' she remembers. "Somehow I just knew He was talking to me."

"No longer just a statue hanging on the cross at church, Jesus became a real and living God to me personally," proclaims Bertina. Almost overnight, she lost interest in the things she had been pursuing to find her identity. "I was beginning to see, hear, feel, and live in a completely different way."

She attended small groups regularly, served in children's ministry, and began to grow deeper in her faith. Despite this reawakening, it wasn't until she decided to be baptized that she found peace that lasted. With her small group, family, and friends she had known since college standing around her, Bertina was baptized. "I felt like I was actually burying a former self."

Now that you've put your trust in me, get ready to go on an adventure, were the words she heard in her heart in that baptism moment. It was an adventure that would become clearer when she joined a team doing an outreach to young people in Times Square. Though she felt stretched out of her comfort zone, she was in her element. "I could see myself doing this every day for the rest of my life."

Bertina felt she had found her vocation: full-time Christian ministry. At first she tried to relegate it to the side while she looked for another career. Then she took a short-term mission trip to Taiwan, which seemed to bring clarity and perspective on how big the world is and how desperate people are to have hope and purpose.

"I returned to New York with a plan to move to Taiwan immediately and become a missionary," she says. A missionary? As she tried to weigh all combinations of options and plans, Bertina only felt more confused, and afraid of making the wrong life decision.

"It was then I realized I was on a journey by faith, which meant taking a leap. Either I follow God or I do things my way. At that moment, I made my decision. I declined a counseling job offer, fell on my face in tears, and began developing a partnership team to empower me to go into full-time ministry."

Obedience requires faith and discipline, Bertina learned firsthand. "But when love takes over, what once seemed like a huge life sacrifice now emerges as an act of obedience and worship, a love offering to God," she explains.

"Some say that the greatest distance is between the head and the heart," Bertina concludes, describing her miracle of a heart healed and a calling discovered. "Within that first year in NYC, my head went on a journey, which led my heart to receive the healing love I had been seeking for so long."

Bertina Hu earned her Master's in School Counseling at New York University, where she also became a follower of Jesus. Trained through the New York Initiative of Every Nation Church, NYC as a campus missionary, the congregation then sent her to Taipei, Taiwan, to help launch a church. She is pursuing work in social entrepreneurship with a passion to reveal the heart of Father God to her generation.

CANILE JACKSON

St. John's University, Queens

Canile Jackson's first time walking into a public school was in 6th grade. The school was near his mother's work in Queens and academically rigorous. By 12 years old, his fellow classmates and so-called friends started to bully him.

Over the next two years, the bullying grew into full-blown colorism (when a person of color with lighter skin exhibits prejudice toward someone with darker skin). Some called him, "Darkness," mimicking a famous comedian's shtick. Canile would pretend to laugh it off, but internally, the repeated jokes and insults cut deep.

He felt lost, ostracized, and insecure, always wondering, "Am I ugly? Unwanted? Can I measure up to anyone?" The cool kids seemed confident and had girlfriends. Why couldn't he be cool and popular enough, or get a girlfriend?

At a young age he was introduced to pornography, which became a reprieve, providing a sense of intimacy. An image of the "ideal woman" formed in his mind and heart. "If I can find her I will be complete," was a frequent thought running through his mind. He attempted to date a girl who he heard liked him, but the relationship quickly fizzled. His insecurity turned into gripping fear, affecting even the things he was skilled at doing. An athlete from his youth, he had real potential to play professional baseball, yet couldn't imagine anything worse than making a mistake in front of a crowd.

He transferred high schools his junior year, trading baseball for football. Yet whatever was once a source of joy had all become drudgery. He started to feel sluggish, down, and unexcited about the future. In his senior year, his coach asked him, "Canile, are you depressed?" Shocked at the candor, he said, "No." Looking back, he knows he was.

By the summer following graduation, Canile was questioning every aspect of his life. Why didn't anything he thought would help actually help? Would he ever be able to sustain a healthy relationship with himself, much less others?

A friend kept encouraging Canile to go to Catholic Mass on Sundays. He enjoyed it and even knelt down, putting a coin in the candle when he prayed, thinking, "This is how I can get some leverage with God." He asked God for help to find himself and to find the right people.

Starting college at St. John's University seemed like the right time to "change everything," including the way he dressed, ate, and spoke. He started to enjoy things again. The desire for the ultimate relationship with the ideal woman remained, though, giving fuel to his private use of porn, which was becoming an addiction. This season of change brought about an invitation to a Christian fellowship gathering on campus, and when Canile arrived this time, he wasn't so afraid. "Their faith is clearly the center of their lives, not a once a week 'drive through,'" Canile remembers thinking.

He became a regular attender, and went with some of his new friends to Every Nation Church, NYC, then subsequently to a conference for college students called Campus Harvest in North Carolina. At the conference, he heard speakers share inspiring truths that impacted him greatly, including Dr. Rice Broocks, author of the book, *God's Not Dead.*

At the end of the conference, Rice invited those who wanted to give everything to God to come to the front of the auditorium. Canile went forward, along with many others. He remembers watching a group of midshipmen from the United States Merchant Marine Academy next to him up front, weeping. "They were big guys in size and stature, way bigger than me," Canile recalls. "Yet in this moment we were all alike—coming to terms with how much we need God in order to find our true identity."

As Canile lingered up front, praying the best he knew how, his life flashed before him. Memories of what he had done, mistakes because of fear, insecurities, and pain all came to mind. These memories were juxtaposed with what he was hearing at the conference, that God loved *him*, and he was a real part of God's family.

"It took me many years to realize my life matters. I found that through surrendering to the power of God, each of us can walk free," Canile says with a quiet confidence. "The injustices, brokenness, and agony we face can lead us through pain into the Truth—the only Truth with power to set us free, and keep us free."

Canile Jackson was born and raised in Queens, New York. He graduated from St. John's University and is a Campus Minister with Every Nation Church, NYC. He devotes his life to helping college students find their purpose through a personal relationship with God.

CORPORATE AND MARKETPLACE

New York, concrete jungle where dreams are made of, there's nothing you can't do.
Jay-Z feat. Alicia Keys, "Empire State of Mind"

Manhattan is a massive global center of marketplace activity. 1.63 million commuters travel to Manhattan every work day, and it is the only borough of NYC that carries the address, New York, NY. It is known as the "heart of the Big Apple," and is the foremost commercial, financial, and cultural hub of the world. With millions working in that core, there is no doubt that the deals and decisions made in NYC affect all aspects of modern life, from smartphones to local schools, from boardrooms to bedrooms.

IN MY OWN WORDS

ELG

The Lamb's Theater and Virgil's Barbecue, Times Square

My move to New York was a total disaster. It was also transformative, redemptive, with just the right amount of paradox. Mine is a story of sin, salvation, dog therapy, and Virgil's barbecue. It is a story only God could write.

I arrived in the city escaping an emotionally and physically abusive husband. In my 20s, I was divorced and broken, concluding I was "soiled for life." On the outside, I was a successful young lawyer, blonde, fun, witty, and well-dressed. On the inside all the voices from my childhood played on repeat at full volume, calling me unworthy, small, cheap trash.

I had left a beautiful row house in Washington, DC, for the quickest sublet I could find—a rat-infested East Village studio. Finding solace in overwork, alcohol abuse, and the arms of nameless, faceless men, I was a mess. What I really needed was a hospital.

My initial connection to Every Nation Church, NYC couldn't have been more nonsensical, but such is the nature of miracles. A friend of mine I knew from the party life (who was known to deal drugs) was on a flight to New York when she saw a passenger reading a Bible. She struck up a conversation with the woman and proceeded to give her *my* email address. The Bible-reading plane passenger was actually a brilliant TV producer who attended Every Nation Church, NYC. She followed through and sent me an email inviting me to join her for a service.

Though I imagined I'd go up in flames the minute I entered a church building, I accepted her offer and walked in the next Sunday night.

It didn't take long to see that lots of people at Every Nation Church, NYC were just as messed up as I was, something I found uniquely compelling and comforting. I concluded it was the hospital I'd been looking for, so I kept going back. As the worship team would sing on those Sunday nights at the Lamb's Theater, I felt like it was heaven. I'd sob at each and every service. The lead pastor, Pastor Ron, made us all laugh and cry, urging us to bow down before a God who truly loved us, broken though we were.

Slowly my provocative clothes, the alcohol, the men, all the worldly pleasures started to lose their appeal. A turning point came the week when one of the pastors spoke prophetic words over me while another prayed. It was then that I was baptized in the Holy Spirit. There in that divinely-appointed "hospital" I was reborn. I marveled at the reality that that one Sunday I walked into church wearing a low-cut Buddha tank top, fresh off a date with my atheist, film-producer fling-of-the-month. And now I was giving my life to Christ. It was a rescue path only God could design.

I started spending time with new, life-giving friends, including Pastor Adam and Susan Burt and their precious daughters. The Burts treated *me* like a daughter, speaking redemptive and supernatural encouragement into my life, though I still had a long way to go. I remember Pastor Adam saying, "One day you will marry a 'tender shepherd', and God will restore the years the locusts have stolen."

The future he was describing sounded quite unappealing at the time, but thankfully, God answers our prayers with the answers we should ask for, instead of what we want in the moment. He also uses others to give us wisdom and a greater vision when we are running short.

Weeks turned into years at this church and served as priceless rehabilitation times under God's umbrella of grace and belonging. I developed a hunger for the Word of God and replaced my dark music collection with praise and worship. Despite my lack of credibility, I helped with a Rutgers University Bible study. I also found a less toxic group of friends—hilarious, kind women. Every Sunday we ate at Virgil's barbecue and prayed together, counseling each other to live holier lives and hold out for God's best.

Eventually I left the hectic law firm where I worked and took on a role that prioritized work-life balance. I also got a rescue dog—an old mutt—for whom Susan Burt knit a pink dog sweater. Her generous act of investing in my sweet dog was, I believe, exactly what Jesus would have done, and recalling this memory makes me cry. Through acts like these I was learning to turn off the nonstop inner voices, realizing God wasn't mad at me. He didn't find me unworthy. He saw me through the lens of His Son and cared about every detail. I was beginning to look people in the eyes without feeling that deep, debilitating shame. I was rescued. I was saved.

All those years earlier, I needed to move to New York City, but God didn't. He has been here since it began. He made a way for me to get to a hospital where He delivered me, miracle after miracle. He used pastors, pastors' wives, a worship team, mentors, friends, and even an old broken-down dog, to shape me into someone redeemed. A woman once so lost became a woman who would lead at her church, host small groups in her home, and start a Christian affinity group at one of the most powerful companies in the world, with her "tender-shepherd" brilliant husband by her side.

I am beyond grateful for those disastrous, paradoxical, transformative, miraculous years in New York City. I will thank Him forever and ever for doing so many miracles in my life.

ELG is a wife, a mother, a small group leader, and an attorney practicing corporate law. Over the years she has grown more liberal in her worship, more conservative in her choice of heels, and recognizes that every behavior makes sense when you really know a person's back story. She finds great encouragement in Christian community.

DAVID MILLER

Midtown Manhattan

David Miller's journey to Manhattan began on a cold, windy day in Dallas, Texas. It was early 1999. Right out of college, he had just started working at his first job at one of the world's largest consulting firms. Though Dallas had much to offer, out of curiosity he had inquired into the new firm's options for an international assignment. "My plan was to spend a few easy weeks in a major city like London or Tokyo," he says. Then, to his surprise, he was offered a year-long role in Manila, Philippines.

He wrestled over the decision to be "on the road," for an entire year, calling it the "biggest decision of my adult life at the time." Pondering his future, he sensed a compelling push, nudging him forward: *Take this assignment in the Philippines, and I will take care of you.*

Two weeks later, he left for Manila, over 8,000 miles away. "The Filipino people were incredibly hospitable and welcoming to me," David remembers. Someone told him about a good place to meet new people, so he visited that place—a church—and even started thinking about a relationship with God for the first time.

After completing his Manila assignment, he was transferred to the Big Apple. "My dream to live in New York was finally happening, and I quickly learned that this was a city that offers a little bit of everything," David recalls.

Since church had become part of his routine, David attended on Sundays, while partying and exploring the bars throughout all five boroughs from Monday to Saturday. "For over a year, I tried to have it both ways—seeking God when I felt abandoned, but turning my back on Him when I didn't. Then, 9/11 changed everything.

On that fateful morning, David arrived early at his midtown office on the 18th floor. He was working to meet a tough deadline, and at first tried to ignore the unusual commotion down the hall.

A colleague compelled him to come see what was happening. "I will always carry with me the trauma of looking out of my office window and my shock at seeing both towers punctured, with plumes of black smoke pouring out of them," David recalls vividly.

It seemed everyone knew someone who was missing. David learned that one of his colleagues tragically lost a fiancé whose office was on the top floor of the second tower. Like many New Yorkers, numbed by the scale of destruction, the next weeks were like living in a haze for David. He resolved one thing, however: "I was determined to get my life right with God, no matter the cost."

The following day, he received an email from a friend in Manila informing him that Every Nation—the group of churches to which his Manila congregation belonged—was responding to the attacks of 9/11 by launching a new church in New York City. David began attending their services, as well as their foundations class, which taught the basics of the Christian life.

Still, he wasn't taking his spiritual life too seriously. "I typically went to happy hour with my coworkers for a few drinks before going to the foundations class," David says. But, when someone started talking about making Jesus Christ not only Savior but Lord of his life things started to sober for him. "This was the missing component of my walk with God," he concluded. "I knew in my heart I had to stop living a double life."

One night, completely broken and alone in his Manhattan apartment, he was ready to make the commitment. David got down on his knees, spoke out loud, and gave everything to God. "I asked Him to do His will in my life, His total and complete will. Immediately, I felt a great weight lift off my shoulders. It was like I was somewhere in nature, breathing the freshest, most pristine air."

The next couple of years became a season of radical spiritual growth. The friendships and environment of Every Nation Church, NYC were helping shape and develop his character and his future.

Within two years, he brought his consulting skills and acumen for leadership to working on the church staff. One of his initial assignments was to field inquiries from people who were interested in relocating to New York. Of the many he talked to, one stood out: Nadia Santiago, a TV reporter from Manila. She felt a strong connection with the victims of 9/11, having just returned weeks earlier from covering a story in Washington, D.C.

David and Nadia discovered that they had attended the same church in Manila for over a year without ever meeting. Soon they met in person in New York, and over time their friendship grew into something deeper.

On September 11, 2005, Pastor Ron Lewis officiated their wedding. "We chose 9/11 as our wedding day as a way to remember the tragedy and celebrate God's redemption in our lives and in the lives of so many New Yorkers,"

David recounts God's sovereign direction and care with gratitude. "Even when I was double-minded, God led me to Manila, and then to NYC, and not just for a career but also for a purpose-filled life."

David Miller graduated from Rice University with honors and from King's University with a Masters of Divinity with high honors. Two years after 9/11, David became the Chief Administrator and Executive Pastor of Every Nation Church, NYC where he served until 2012. With his wife, Nadia, and three children, he is back in Dallas, the very place where his miracle in Manhattan began.

NATALIE CHODNIEWICZ

Virgil's Barbecue, Times Square

"Church is mostly for older people or parents with young children," Natalie Chodniewicz decided in her early 20's. She took a marketing job after graduation and moved to New York City from the Midwest and there she stopped attending church altogether.

A focused achiever at work, she led a team that sold advertising on the lit-up billboards of Broadway and midtown Manhattan, mere steps from where the famous ball drops at midnight early New Year's Eve. Her professional life was on the upswing, just like her designer handbags. "I was single in Manhattan, dating regularly, traveling the world, and happy on the outside," she says. "Inside, though, I felt increasingly isolated and alone."

Natalie's father, whom she adored, had died a few years earlier from a sudden heart attack at age 47. This left her fearing what the future might bring. She found herself drawn to men who shunned commitment and showed disrespect, or worse. One long-term relationship abruptly ended when the man who told her he loved her stole her identity and tens of thousands of dollars.

The morning of September 11, 2001, brought a devastating blow to the heart and soul of the nation, shrouding people's day-to-day existence with fear and uncertainty, including her own. She had watched the events unfold from the 14th floor of her office in Times Square.

"9/11 made me terrified of living in Manhattan," she recalls. "I felt paralyzed most days, wondering what was coming next. I attended several work seminars teaching employees how to live with fear and anxiety," Natalie remembers. "I was searching desperately for peace."

A colleague from work invited her to attend a new church just starting to meet at the Lamb's Theater, near her office. "On my very first visit, I was impacted in a dramatic way," Natalie says. One of the leaders invited her to join their group for lunch at Virgil's BBQ near the theater.

"Rice Broocks turned to me and asked a simple question, 'How are you *really* doing Natalie?' So I shared how I was paralyzed from fear and didn't know how to manage. He gave me a verse from the Bible, writing it down on a napkin. It was one I remembered vaguely from growing up in Sunday school, and it said, "God has not given you a spirit of fear, but a spirit of love, and of power, and a sound mind." (2 Timothy 1:7)

From that moment on, Natalie started learning how to overcome fear. "I carried that verse on the napkin and memorized it, declaring it to be true in every category of my life every day," she remembers. "I was learning practical ways of applying scripture to my life, ways that helped radically change the way I was thinking, feeling, and living." God's intervention in Natalie's soul caused her to start making different life choices. "Slowly," she says, "the inner pieces of my heart that had been wandering for so long began to find solace, peace, and love like I had never experienced. It felt like a miraculous transformation."

Natalie made many new friends in her church community, friends with whom she shared hobbies and deeply admired. While dating had been an integral part of her life and identity up to this point, she now committed to waiting for a man she could truly trust, someone who, like her, wanted to live fearlessly.

Little did she know that when she married her husband, Josh Chodniewicz, who she met through a church connection, they would embark on just such a fearless journey together. They left NYC after 10 years for a new adventure in Texas, one demanding many more bold steps of faith.

A cheerleading accident back in college left Natalie with a horrific skull fracture, the kind from which nine out of ten people die. The doctors told her she would likely never have children, or if she did, her pregnancies would be difficult. Nonetheless, Natalie got pregnant, only to lose the baby through ectopic pregnancy. Still boldly declaring the scriptures, she got pregnant again, not just once but three more times, bringing her and Josh three beautiful sons.

Following her third pregnancy, just days after delivery, Natalie was rushed to the hospital with post-partum hemorrhaging. After nine blood transfusions and multiple abdominal surgeries, it's a miracle she made it out alive. "The Christian religion," Natalie says with strong conviction, "is not a 'rule book' meant to make us seek a life of perfection. Rather, it's a *living* book, filled with power and promises for miracles, so many that I've needed over and over again."

She describes her life today as "beauty sprung from the ashes," and her time in New York City as a turning point. "I will never forget God's pursuit of me during that season of 9/11, how He healed my heart and made me fearless, as the woman, wife, and mother I am today."

Natalie Chodniewicz worked for over a decade in advertising and marketing in managing the largest digital signage in Times Square for Thompson Reuters and Nasdaq. Alongside her husband, Josh, she is a corporate professional, a mom to three sons, and a successful creator and author of the children's book and gratitude activity, Popcorn Thanks.

TIFFANY DEGENNARO

Fifth Avenue, Midtown Manhattan

Tiffany Degennaro's upbringing was rough, to say the least. Raised by a violent, alcoholic father and a mother who spent most of her time either running from her past or escaping from her future, Tiffany felt like she was "raised by wolves consumed by their own personal demons."

In her own eyes her life was miserable, probably because "she wasn't good enough, didn't deserve better, and was a horrible sinner." Tiffany attributes a lot of her guilt to a parochial school and church upbringing, where she was baptized as a newborn. "I knew who God was, but never came close to really getting to know Him," she describes. "Our relationship was strictly religious."

She spent her early years going to church, receiving the sacraments, praying, and performing all of the Catholic rituals. Yet through all of this, nothing changed. Her only answer was to get out of Brooklyn. "I thought if I moved to Manhattan, I could start over," Tiffany recalls.

Her brother, who had recently married and moved to Manhattan, kept asking her to go with him to a well-known Protestant church. She finally relented. Sitting there, Tiffany wondered, *What is it about this church? Is it a cult? Why is everyone so happy when they sing? Why don't I have that? If my own father doesn't love me, then how can God love me?* These questions and others kept running through her mind. She felt like the pastor knew all of her secrets too. "His sermons seemed personally written for me."

Tiffany was desperate for acceptance, but the church service made her feel even more alienated. "I'm not a goodie two-shoes, I don't feel 'holy' or saved; I'm not wearing Laura Ashley flowered dresses or the perfect hairdo. I'm a punk-rock art student. These people will never get me," she concluded.

Meanwhile, a cacophony of voices kept rattling off inside her head, making her feel more and more horrible every day. Each morning she would wake up thinking, "I should just leave this place for good, since my life has no value."

Years of depression followed, culminating in one fateful day when she nearly succumbed to suicidal thoughts. At that moment, on her 26th birthday, Tiffany cried out to God. She confessed her brokenness and pleaded with Him. She just couldn't take it anymore.

In that horrific moment, a sincere and loving voice peacefully took center stage in her mind. *I have not forgotten you. As many tears as you have cried, multiply that number by the highest number imaginable. That's how many tears I've shed for you, because I love you and I want you to have a better life. Give your old life to me and I'll give a new one to you.*

Always the sarcastic native New Yorker, Tiffany said in response, "I guess that's what it means to be born again?" And with joy she felt his response back to her, *Yes, my daughter, that's it!*

While so much changed for her, Tiffany would go through many more difficult seasons since that day more than 20 years ago. On 9/11, she lost many friends and family members working in the towers. Other family members never fully recovered. She has endured a total of 23 sinus surgeries from breathing in toxins from Ground Zero where the towers collapsed. Though surgeons said she would never smell again Tiffany declares, "The Lord healed me!"

She lost most of her personal resources along with her business during the collapse of the banks in 2008. Amidst huge financial losses and massive bills from the IRS, she also experienced failed relationships, career changes, and losing friends with whom she worked to suicide. "This list, believe it or not," says Tiffany, "is just the tip of the iceberg." Despite all this trauma, she knows with a deep, clear certainty that God has been by her side through all of it. Every hardship and challenge has made her who she is today, and she wouldn't change any aspect of her journey, even if she could.

Pastor Ron Lewis, who is married to her dear friend Lynette, baptized Tiffany for the second time as an adult at Every Nation Church, NYC. She knows with confidence she is loved. After many years of being single, she married a childhood friend from Brooklyn who pursued her and won her heart. "Not only am I loved, I'm also so very blessed!" Tiffany says with her famous red-lipstick smile.

She loves her job and loves building a team she can pour into. She is vice president of the number one prestige beauty brand in the world, and has worked with some of the most well-known figures in the fashion industry. No matter where Tiffany goes or what she does, she has a devoted family of believers who care deeply and unconditionally for her. They know her inside and out and love her as she is.

"So, what are you waiting for?" Tiffany poses to those still on the fence. "You've got nothing to lose and everything to gain. We are all beautiful disasters and works in progress. You will have trials and challenges no matter what. You can't control your life; believe me, I've tried. This Brooklyn girl is one tough cookie. But if I couldn't handle it, not many can. How about letting God carry you through it and take control of it? Fall into His arms—you won't regret it."

Tiffany Degennaro is a proud native New Yorker who is Brooklyn strong! She is a lover of all things in fashion and beauty and runs retail stores for the #1 prestige beauty brand.

SOLOMON CHOI

Chelsea and Times Square

March 2008 was not exactly the best time to relocate to New York City. The financial capital of the world was experiencing tremors—major banks were going bankrupt, the stock market was losing trillions in value, and multiple industries were requiring a federal bailout of historic proportions.

Solomon Choi, an entrepreneur who grew up in the restaurant industry, had just arrived from California. His vision was to create the best frozen dessert experience he could for New Yorkers in the city's first self-serve frozen yogurt shop. He opened his first store, "16 Handles," in July 2008, in the middle of the financial crisis, believing what looked like *bad* timing could actually be the *best* timing.

Thousands of rave reviews from customers, and more than 30 stores later, the pioneering "fro-yo" shop is now a certified NYC success story. A dozen years almost to the day from his first store opening, the COVID-19 pandemic brought Solomon his toughest business challenge to date. "Like most others, we were forced to shut down in March 2020," he recounts. "Almost all of our stores were closed, minimally for a month, with no business."

The "high-touch" model that had set the business apart was now a misfit in a world where many thought a viral pathogen could spread through surfaces. It was a time of serious uncertainty, he remembers. "I even had some franchisees who gave up and said there was no way we were going to rebound, that no one would ever come into our stores again."

The concerns were not unfounded. By December 2020, 2,800 businesses in NYC had permanently closed. One of them included the famed bar Tonic, located in Times Square, which closed down due to the pandemic after a successful run of 16 years. This left Tonic's owners with a supply of restaurant equipment they had to liquidate.

"My franchisee was buying freezers from Tonic," Solomon recalls, "when I received an email from a broker offering a space where a now-closed frozen yogurt shop had been. It was on 7th Avenue, two doors up from the 'M&M's World' store in Times Square."

Solomon forwarded the email to his franchisee whom he thought would be interested in such a prime location. With foot traffic low during COVID-19 and the ensuing drop in the real estate market, the franchisee received an extraordinary deal in an area that was previously unattainable for him, and in May 2021, fourteen months after the pandemic started, another 16 Handles store opened in the heart of Times Square, fully compliant with the CDC, the Centers for Disease Control and Prevention.

Discovering opportunities where everyone else sees obstacles is nothing new to Solomon. He actually considers it part of the narrative of his life and gives credit to God. "Often, we are best able to see the miraculous in hindsight, recognizing what has transpired and knowing it should have been impossible," he states. "These are the moments that simply could not happen without the grace of God and his direct intervention in my life and business."

Divine leading has given him foresight as well. Prior to the public health crisis, Solomon and his company were "planting seeds" to grow their technology. "When the pandemic started we had already built an exceptional online platform," he said. The company's app and website permitted customers to order digitally from the stores.

Thanks to this technological infrastructure, his company continued to do business and actually prospered during the pandemic. In fact, just four months after COVID-19 restrictions were put in place, in August 2020 yet another new store opened in the iconic Manhattan neighborhood of Tribeca. *Yahoo Finance*'s Seana Smith described the company's unique growth as, "doing something not many in the industry are doing at this time in the midst of the pandemic. They are expanding."

As for so many, 2020 was a year filled with moments of discouragement, trepidation, and fear of the unknown for Solomon and his business. Even so, he marvels at how successful and sustained their business model has been. "My wife and I talk frequently about how this business is bigger than we are, because it's really about God's kingdom. My burning desire has always been to build a platform for His purpose. We are in this to bring glory to Him."

Solomon Choi is the founder and CEO of 16 Handles, New York City's largest frozen dessert brand. He graduated from the University of Southern California, and moved to NYC in 2008. Solomon is married to Hannah Chang and they have two children, Jubilee and Joshua.

DEE RIVERA

The Bronx

Dee Rivera's website describes in beautiful language a magazine she created in 2005, called *Latinista.* It is also a fitting description of Dee herself:

> *"... the Latina woman who sets the direction of her own life and lives it to its fullest on her own terms. Her point-of-view is unmistakably American, her culture is full of color, food, and music, unwavering in optimism and wide open to great things ahead."*

Dee *is* a Latinista, but her life and journey were not always so glamorous.

She grew up near Yankee Stadium in the Bronx, with a strong Catholic upbringing woven through many generations of Puerto Ricans. Even as a tender four-year-old, she asked sincere questions and longed to know her purpose. "I had a calling," she remembers, and also felt, "There's something very specific for me to do."

Through the sacrifices of her parents and grandparents, she attended private Catholic schools, until college. Four years at Hunter College in Manhattan led to a move to England, where she studied journalism and architecture. With relentless passion and energy, plus a knack for reaching the masses, she wondered for many years, "What exactly is truth?" Her search led her to a church that, at first glance, seemed committed to revealing truth and the purpose she longed to know.

The activities and beliefs of this congregation appealed to her in many ways. In true Dee style, she dove in head first and brought her energy and love for people to church every Sunday and often on weekdays too. "I was committed," she remembers. "These were my people and I was all in."

As the years went on and Dee's career was growing, when it came to her church she had countless indications and questions about her church that were deeply worrisome. 16 years would go by before she could no longer resist the thought she had been ignoring for so long—"I am connected to a cult."

Up to 10,000 cults exist in the United States today, and Dee couldn't believe she was in one of them. Her conclusion matched the description though: "a social group defined by its unusual religious, spiritual, or philosophical beliefs, or by its common interest in a particular personality, object, or goal."

She spent years trying to deny it because, in her words, "Ours was not one that harmed people physically or sexually, but a more subtle cult that abused people through the dangerous misuse of the Bible to control its members," she explains. "Many of us were enamored with the leaders and their passion. Whatever they asked for we would give, even when something didn't feel right."

"Interaction with a cult begins very slowly," Dee goes on to say. She compares it to an abusive marriage. "No one goes into it thinking they're marrying someone abusive. The control starts slowly and methodically, and after a while, you simply think it's normal," she says.

It was her personal relationship with God that empowered her to leave that church eventually and get free. "It took me years to get it all straightened out," she says. "I wasn't so much mad at God, but angry at the people."

She now faced the choice of staying away from church entirely or searching for a new congregation. "Since Jesus loves the church and calls it His bride, I need to love her too," she concluded. "I also value accountability and doing life with friends who are intently pursuing God." As she visited other churches around the city, Dee felt continually drawn to one in particular. Someone invited her to the church's women's conference where she was impressed by the pastor's wife, a corporate woman like Dee herself. "This woman was sharing about her long journey of waiting for a husband, how she never gave up and kept enduring. The whole time I kept thinking, 'I can relate to this woman. She 'gets it' and is so much like me."

For the next two years, Dee sat at the back of the auditorium on 96th Street and 3rd Avenue where the church was meeting. She was observing, making sure it would be a safe place. "These people seem 'normal' and trustworthy," she thought. Finally, she approached the pastor after a service and asked, "Who holds you accountable?" A bit taken off guard, he looked at her with kindness and began listing the individuals on his accountability team. As Dee told him about her background, he asked if they could pray together, which she welcomed. "I think from that point on I realized not all church leaders are stuck on themselves," Dee says with a note of humor.

"One of the best gifts I received from this new church was experiencing the Holy Spirit," Dee recalls. "In the Bible He's known as 'the Counselor.' I need counsel and help every day, not just from a therapist whom I make an appointment to see, but from God's own Spirit who is *with* me and *in* me," she says.

Dee summarizes it all by saying, "I've found my purpose as an entrepreneur with creative projects happening all the time. But the miracles unfold at the crossroads when we make the choice to cling to God and keep walking, rather than turn out of hurt and give in. No matter what success I have or don't have, my decision is firmly made. I'll never let go of God. He is the only One who is truly perfect, so I'm holding on to Him!"

Dee Rivera is the CEO of DCG Media Group and manages lifestyle brands globally. She is currently launching her second book, A Right To Shoes, and is living her best life.

BIJOU

Federal Plaza Immigration Court, Manhattan

Certain landmarks in the city of New York go completely unnoticed, even to its natives. One of them is 26 Federal Plaza. It's the building where millions of immigrants come to make their naturalization dreams come true. For Bijou, it would become a symbol of disappointment and pain.

Half Igbo, half Yoruba, Bijou was born in London, grew up in Lagos, Nigeria, was reared in boarding school, and found herself in NYC ready to attend university at the age of 15. Her aunt, who lived in Brooklyn, agreed to adopt her legally so she could transition to life in America. "Adoption is a common method of naturalization for a minor," Bijou explains. But what started as a straightforward legal process, would soon become a 20-year journey filled with bureaucracy and shame.

Immigration officers ensure all documentation in these cases is legitimate and meets the criteria. Bijou was told her process through the system would likely take a year. Instead, the officer assigned to her case instantly had suspicions of the adoption legality and, after several interviews, decided to launch an investigation.

"This immigration uncertainty became a testing ground for my faith right from the start," Bijou remembers. "What we initially thought would go quickly now spanned eight years with no real end in sight."

Meanwhile, her first job was as a Junior Economic Advisor for the Nigerian Commission to the United Nations. Unsatisfied, even though her masters was in Public Affairs from Columbia, Bijou decided on a career in fashion instead. Focused from the start, she knew about hard work and determination, traits that would become essential for the challenges to come.

Finally, she got the news that although the adoption had now been deemed legal, the officer didn't find her application substantial enough to grant her permanent residency. She had waited eight years only to have her case denied.

This denial wasn't the first. There had been two others prior and each time Bijou's aunt would appeal. This time the denial was final. It came with a notice of deportation. No more appeals. No more options. Bijou would have to leave the country she called home.

"Fortunately, through character references, I was able to stay in the U.S., but now without 'status,'" Bijou explains. "Status meant that although I already had a full-time job, at any moment I could lose my position and be unable to work until the system figured out what to do with me."

Her case seemed so hopeless by now that even her attorney was encouraging her to get married, not for love but for legal status. She rejected that and stayed constantly worried about what having "no status" meant for the future. While her career path was bringing promotions and success, she just kept praying for a miracle.

By this time, there was no telling what had become of her application. "Now I was the one asking the Lord to send me a man of God who I could marry," Bijou laughs and remembers. "It seemed at this point like my only way out, or rather in!"

Then the laws of the land suddenly changed. The Obama Administration issued what was known as DACA—a law allowing children who had come to the U.S. before the age of 16 to qualify for protected status. "DACA gave me a glimmer of hope and bought more time," says Bijou. "I was able to stay and get a legal working document. Only then did my employer ask for updated identification—after five years on the job!" The timing wasn't lost on Bijou. Still curious why her original application had never been processed, she inquired one last time, only to discover it had been locked away *for years* at a center for finalized cases.

She had spent tens of thousands of dollars to go through a legal system that had failed her, but Bijou's story was not over yet. "Each time I reached a dead-end, God would send another provision," she says. Six more years would pass until on June 11, 2021, Bijou would go back to 26 Federal Plaza, stand by the American flag, and officially become a citizen of the United States of America.

Her miracles spanned the course of 20 years filled with many moments of despair and hopelessness. "Reading the Bible has always helped me," says Bijou, "because it's filled with stories of so many people who face struggles worse than mine, and persevere."

Two verses were especially personal to her during her arduous journey: 2 Chronicles 20:12, "Our God, will you not judge them? For we have no power to face this vast army that is attacking us. We do not know what to do, but our eyes are on you." And Psalm 126:1, "When the Lord restored the fortunes of Zion, we were like those who dreamed."

In the days when Bijou had no idea what to do, her eyes remained on God. Finally, when He answered her prayers for citizenship, it happened so quickly, it felt like a dream.

Bijou A. currently heads up data strategy for a leading cosmetic retailer. She's had a 14-year career in the fashion and beauty industry and recently became an alumna of Harvard Business School. She's a proud member of Every Nation Church, NYC and loves spending time with friends and family.

THE NATIONS

Give me your tired, your poor, your huddled masses yearning to breathe free, The wretched refuse of your teeming shore. Words engraved on the pedestal of the Statue of Liberty from the 1883 sonnet, *The New Colossus,* by Emma Lazarus

New York City is the melting pot of the world. More than 36% of its population is born outside the United States; countless millions stopover in NYC on their way to positions of leadership and influence in their home nations—hundreds of presidents and diplomats studied or worked in NYC long before they were elected or appointed. The most linguistically diverse city in the world, at least 700 languages are spoken daily in NYC, and for millions, the journey coming to America begins here.

IN MY OWN WORDS

Alex Meltsin

Brighton Beach, Brooklyn

To escape the hardships of Communism and antisemitism, my Jewish family emigrated from the Soviet Union to the United States in 1989 when I was just 11 years old.

Glasnost—which roughly translates as "openness" in Russian—was President Gorbachev's sweeping reform that opened up the country and normalized international travel. Hundreds of thousands of us made the difficult journey from our homes to the United States for what we thought would be a much better life. Though that hope was eventually realized, it would take a long time.

Growing up in Brooklyn wasn't easy. I was the youngest in a single-parent household and my mother worked from morning to evening to provide for my older brother, my grandfather, and me. Pizza for dinner was a luxury, as we couldn't usually afford to splurge on take-out. Living in poverty, we shared our apartment with roaches, mice, and rats. Our first set of furniture was not Early American or French Provincial. It was "Great Depression," straight from Brooklyn's garbage bins.

In high school and college, pained and disillusioned, I looked for escape. I spent my days hanging out with the wrong crowd, using drugs. One night after a round of angel dust—PCP, a drug sometimes used to tranquilize elephants and a very dangerous hallucinogenic—I felt like I was having a nervous breakdown. I walked the streets of Bayridge and suddenly began crying out to God. I had no real connection to God outside of hearing other people speak of Him. This was an act of stoned desperation. When I got home, I went to sleep.

The next day, I woke up sober—completely free from hallucinations caused by my addiction. In shock, I knew then for a fact that God had in fact answered my prayer.

I began attending a Russian Messianic Church, but not because of my recent God-encounter. I went to church simply because of my new girlfriend, Sasha. Sasha and I met in college, partying, drinking, and chasing anything that could numb the pain. The church we attended in Brooklyn was providentially co-founded with the assistance and mentoring of Pastor Ron Lewis from Every Nation Church, NYC, and was led by Juri Popov. It has helped tens of thousands of Russian emigres over the course of its existence, more than half of whom were Jews.

When Sasha got pregnant—prior to our marriage—we initially thought we might do what many of our friends had done: abort the baby. Thankfully, Pastor Juri consulted with us and we decided against abortion. Later a leader gave me the entire offering from one of the church services. I'm not sure he was supposed to do that, but it felt to me like a personal demonstration of God's love for my family.

I came to Christ at the age of twenty and married Sasha soon after. We continued to live in sin, do drugs, and stay messed up, but God began to work in us. My wife and I were changing, and with all personal transformation comes trials and tribulations. I was rarely in church due to the tension it created with my Jewish family and meanwhile, our friends had disowned us because we had stopped doing drugs. My Christian life was filled with ups and downs—I underwent a severe ordeal that put my faith on the line. I was questioning God and the church. I could barely function.

Out of the blue, right when I needed it the most, I received a text message from Pastor Ron that I have saved to this day. I knew God was speaking directly to me as soon as I read it: "It's not easy, but I ask you to trust Jesus in this difficult situation. I'm asking you to walk with the Lord and trust Him. Jesus is the head of his church. You don't need to focus on that. You are a great man of God, and the Lord will NOT fail or forsake you. I am trusting His grace to touch your life. Be patient; He is coming through for you. Much love my friend and peace to your soul (John 14:27)."

I persisted and continued to grow in the Lord. God blessed me. My business was booming, and my wife Sasha graduated from the prestigious New York University at the top of her class.

Today, Sasha, our daughters and I live in a beautiful home near the beach, and Sasha is now a dental hygienist and office manager. Over the years, we have been honored to help many others become disciples of Jesus. In 2017, I sensed a calling to start a church and become a pastor, and I am pursuing that with all my energy.

The scripture reveals God's pursuit of us in Romans 5:8: "But God demonstrates his own love for us in this: While we were still sinners, Christ died for us." As a Russian Jew, I am so grateful to have been able to press through hardship and come to a place of freedom, security, and beauty. Despite the difficulties, coming to America turned out to be a great thing, but stepping into the kingdom of God was infinitely greater.

Alex Meltsin is the husband to Sasha, a graduate of New York University, and they have two daughters. They live in a beautiful home in Seagate, Brooklyn. Alex founded and owns an environmental company and is also the leader of Every Nation Church, NYC's Brooklyn campus.

EMMA

Her bodega, New York City

Emma was born and raised in Bangladesh in a Muslim family. Along with her husband, also raised Muslim, Emma came to America in 1999, and together they opened a bodega in the heart of New York City.

Their business kept them extremely busy, but Emma still wanted to practice her Islamic faith regularly and faithfully. "My deepest desire at that time was to serve Allah, be a good Muslim, and live worthy of heaven," she recalls. Her husband, for his part, never paid much attention to religion.

One day Emma told her husband she wanted to practice Islam more intentionally. "Can I take some time out of the workday to pray and do what our religion requires?" she asked. "We came to America to earn money, not to practice Islam," he answered. "If you want to be a strict Muslim, you will have to stay at home." For him, living the proverbial "American Dream" was everything. This meant that Emma, out of respect for her husband, needed to work long hours every day at their bodega, usually from open to close.

One night, with fear in her heart and tears in her eyes, over an ongoing sense of falling short, she prayed, "Oh my Lord, I'm a sinful servant. How can all my sin be forgiven before death?" For the next month she prayed and fasted, asking God, "Please let me serve you. My husband must have a heart to let me serve you, Allah."

When the month was over, Emma politely asked her husband again for the flexibility to make time to practice religion, but his heart was unchanged. She was devastated and became very angry. "I'm praying, I'm calling, but Allah is not listening. Am I doing something wrong? Or is there a much bigger problem?"

Every prayer Emma prayed seemed met with silence. So from that night on, she chose not to pray to Allah any longer. She still believed in a divine creator, and in life after death, but she no longer believed in the Muslim God as she had long understood him.

Emma offered one last prayer. "I do not know who You are. What is Your name that I can call upon You? Show me the straight path so I can go to You. I need You to forgive all my sins so I can be in Your presence."

The day after this prayer, there was a knock on the door of her apartment. Looking through the peephole she saw a man and a woman she didn't recognize. "I remembered my husband's requirement to 'never open the door to a stranger.'" Then Emma heard a more powerful voice in her heart, saying, *Open the door and talk to them.* She unlocked the door with caution, chatted for a few minutes, then invited them in.

"What is your religion?" they asked. "That's a strange question," Emma thought to herself. She considered telling them what she had just told Allah: that she did not believe in his religion, that she had just asked the true creator, whoever He was, to show her the right path. "I was beginning to wonder if the creator was answering my prayer by sending someone to my door."

Still, she was afraid, so she responded simply, "I am a Muslim." The man asked Emma if she had ever read the Bible. She said she hadn't but mentioned that she would be interested in reading it if it was written in Bengali.

A week later the stranger returned with exactly what she had requested, a Bengali Bible. The miraculous interaction that started with a door-knock was beginning a monumental change in Emma's life. She knew with conviction, God had heard her prayer. Emma began reading the Bible with fervency in the days that followed. She felt like God Himself was speaking to her. Reading the words of Jesus from John 14, she spoke them aloud:

> *I am the way, and the truth, and the life. No one comes to the Father except through me...Peace I leave with you; my peace I give to you. Not as the world gives do I give to you. Let not your hearts be troubled, neither let them be afraid.*

These words brought deep peace to her soul. Rather than a rigid code of ethics, she found the words to be powerful and life-giving.

After a few years of friendship and more conversations with the man and woman who came to her door, Emma became a believer in Jesus. For the first time in her life, she was confident in the knowledge that she was eternally forgiven.

"God canceled out all my sins and set me free," she shares with a glimmer in her eyes. Now I have lasting joy and peace. I live a new life, because of what Jesus did on the cross. I feel no guilt because I have no guilt. He took it away. When I die someday, I have assurance I will live with God and His son Jesus for eternity, not because of anything I have done, but by the grace of God alone."

Emma is now a woman with a mission. Her passion is to share God's love through words and good deeds in all five boroughs.

Emma and her husband own a small bodega in the city, open seven days a week, 12 hours a day. They have two grown children, one who works in New York City and another who is studying at a private university.

IAN WANG

Former American Bible Society, Lincoln Square

Ian Wang was born and raised in Chengdu, the capital of the Sichuan province of China, the hometown of adorable pandas and spicy hot pot. Before arriving in New York City in 2001, Chinese culture and Communist doctrines influenced his world view, in particular, the belief of Confucianism that "a just cause should be pursued for the common good."

Ian believed in the moral and practical duty of each citizen of a society to champion these ideals, so while he was enjoying the freedom and ingenuity of the United States, he was also troubled by inequality and injustice he observed. He was equally frustrated by what he perceived as his own inability to advocate or promote meaningful change.

An equity analyst working in finance, he was shocked by the discrimination and prejudice he witnessed against the Asian American and Pacific Islander community and other minority groups, even in his prestigious firm. With no relatives nearby or any chance to visit his parents, the burden of isolation, loneliness and homesickness also weighed heavily on him.

It was around Christmastime, when a friend of a friend's, Diane, invited him to church. Going to church seemed "so American" to Ian. Curious, he started to explore God, treating the encouraging messages he heard at church like self-help speeches from Tony Robbins, which he had often used to learn English.

Though initially a skeptic, he now found himself being drawn as he watched people socializing around free food and helping each other with real-life issues. Impressed by the altruistic behaviors he was seeing in both the locals and internationals, he immediately said yes when asked to volunteer, surmising it was the least he could do according to the Chinese cultural norm of reciprocity.

Serving and being part of this community now had him examining more deeply his cultural values and social beliefs, questioning his own identity as an atheist. Ian was intently listening to passionate messages and worship songs, surprised to experience emotions for the God he did not know.

He joined a "Connect Group" and found not only space to learn more about being a Christian, but a place to develop real friendships. Potlucks, game nights, and hiking trips meant he was no longer isolated and alone. Strangely, he even started feeling like he belonged.

Now volunteering for the Food and Beverage Team with Nadine, an American brought up in Germany, went beyond just offering food and drinks to "preparing a table to welcome the city," as they called it. New visitors each week reminded Ian of himself.

His early exploratory attendance and curiosity had now brought Ian to a unique Sunday evening service in the Lincoln Square area, when something entirely unplanned happened.

As the message came to a close, Pastor Ron asked people to close their eyes. Then he said, "Those who are willing to accept Jesus Christ as your Lord and Savior and follow God's plan, please stand up."

Ian heard people clapping and cheering loudly around him. When he opened his eyes he couldn't believe that he was standing! It wasn't until two days later, after receiving a congratulatory message from Diane, who had first invited him to church, that he fully grasped the significance of his decision to stand that night. He concluded it was the Holy Spirit who had compelled him in that moment to stand. Ian had taken a stand that night, and the transformation of his life and identity had only begun.

To help others belong and grow deeper, he started a Connect Group, co-leading with Nadine. Leading together, they appreciated how much they shared in their worldview, despite their obvious differences in upbringing and culture. After making countless pots of coffee together and leading many Bible studies for others, Ian and Nadine decided to get married.

Today, they are living in NYC, still active in their church and grateful to be building a community filled with so much diversity. When Ian sees inequality and racial injustice, he still feels sad and angry, yet he recognizes the universal need of every human heart to be changed through the gospel. He values the fact that the church has historically been at the forefront of social reform, and finds fulfillment in being a change agent in his own work and circles of influence.

"We can all remain intimidated by division and death or, as Jesus showed us, we can shake off the grave clothes and experience a resurrection," Ian emphasizes. He marvels at his journey that started out so lonely and isolated, and now, personally and geographically, feels like coming home.

Ian Wang came to the United States from China in 2000 to attend college, later deciding to make New York City his home. He works as an investment advisor and promotes understanding and cooperation between nations.

YUTO MATSUMOTO

The Empire State Building

It was the handshake that changed his life, and it happened to an unlikely man, from an unlikely nation, at a very unlikely moment.

Yuto Matsumoto, a Japanese businessman and chemist who worked for one of the most esteemed companies in his nation, was simply looking forward to a day with his daughter. Nao, his daughter, was a new Christian. She just arrived in the U.S. from Japan to get some time with her dad, something not all young women are prone to want, especially when just arriving in New York City. Yuto was planning to take Nao out for some lunch and afternoon shopping, but she said she would rather spend time with "her people."

"Whoever they are," Yuto thought. Nonetheless, he followed Nao's lead. They took a short subway ride to meet up with some young adults at The King's College, at that time located in the Empire State Building.

As they walked into a conference room, it was Pastor Ron Lewis who first greeted Yuto, sensing that he, like Ron, was a bit out of place among this 20-something crowd. Ron was there with his own son Nathan and a few of Nathan's friends. Moments later, all the kids had tickets to go up on the observation deck, while the two dads found themselves left alone in the conference room. Wanting to engage the Japanese father, Ron asked what he thought about Nao's new faith and religion. Yuto replied, “I’m a not-so-enthusiastic Buddhist who believes in my own ability to master my destiny.”

Struck by this response, Ron invited Yuto to an eight-hour seminar on the Christian faith he was conducting a few days later, to be followed by a viewing of the film *The Passion of the Christ.* At the nudging of Nao, Yuto agreed to attend.

Sitting through the Biblical foundations seminar, Yuto found it intriguing. Later he felt similarly engaged while watching the epic film about the crucifixion of Jesus Christ. When the movie ended, Yuto patiently waited in the back row until the crowd had exited and he saw Ron heading for the door. They shook hands.

“Something consumed me right then,” Yuto recalls. “I burst into tears, my nose running. I was also sweating and shaking. I didn't know what was happening to me. But now I know—I was being touched by the Holy Spirit.”

Preparing for a business trip to Japan a few days later, Yuto discovered a letter his daughter had left for him. In it, she tenderly wrote:

> “I want to tell you how I respect you for everything. Who you are, and who you are becoming. I'm excited to see what God does in your life. Try to give God a try. Just give it a try to go to church and meet “your people.” Pastor Ron is your friend and he's always here for you. Eventually God will reveal Himself to you. You will receive Him.”

Stirred by his daughter’s words, Yuto began studying the Christian faith with focus and fervency. As a man of science he had many questions, yet he studied and also took action.

While in Yokohama he attended Nao’s church where he found himself listening to a sermon about Jesus on the cross. Now he was weeping again. When the service was over, he approached the pastor and asked what he must do. "All my questions are not yet answered," Yuto told him, "but I think my soul and my heart are crying out for help."

He returned home to NYC and was sensing it was time to be baptized. He connected again with Pastor Ron, who told him that some of his friends from the New York church as well as from Yokohama, were all going to attend a global church conference in Los Angeles. It seemed to Yuto like a perfect time and place to be baptized.,

When the day came, Yuto was nervous. He was up early reading scripture to calm himself, and happened upon the passage in Matthew 3 when Jesus was baptized and, "the Holy Spirit descended upon him like a dove." This comforted Yuto and he felt ready.

Pastor Ron baptized Yuto in the hotel swimming pool with friends and family watching. Emerging from the water, wiping his wet face with a towel, Yuto looked up and saw not one, but three doves flying over their heads. Two landed atop the building next to them, while the other white dove fluttered just over the pool as if to linger, with the shimmering light of the Los Angeles morning sun behind its wings. It was not only beautiful; it was spectacular. Yuto knew God was near and felt His blessing as his morning reading remarkably aligned with his baptism experience.

Miraculous signs and wonders were just beginning. Yuto had once been married but he and his wife had been divorced for more than a decade. The divorce resulted in bitterness and pain for years. Now his former wife, Nao's mother Takako, had also become a Christian believer. She was privately working through her bitterness against Yuto when the two connected with each other and agreed to meet to make amends. It was difficult, but they were able to talk about how they hurt each other, after which they both apologized. In that moment, love between them seemed to return suddenly, unexpectedly, and miraculously. Very soon after their talk, to the surprise of their two children and others, they decided to remarry and rewrite their family story.

There was more. Yuto and Takako had a son, Kazuyoshi, who had literally disappeared over a year earlier while attending college in Hawaii. Their hearts had been in anguish not knowing his whereabouts or why he refused to contact them. Miraculously, he too encountered Jesus and is now married to a pastor's daughter, preaching and serving on the staff of a church in Nagoya, Japan.

Gradually, each member of the Matsumoto family was touched by God. Yuto says in his calm confident smile with eyes that gleam, "He has saved and restored us."

It was just as his young teenage daughter had written to him: "Eventually God will reveal Himself to you. You will receive Him."

Yuto Matsumoto is a scientist, chemist, businessman, and the CEO of Hodogaya Chemical. He married Takako in 1985. They divorced in 2000, and remarried each other in 2009. They currently live in Tokyo with their dog and enjoy their children and grandchildren.

AZIZ AND MADINA SAMIROV

A small park in Forest Hills, Queens

The ancient town of Samarkand, situated in the Central Asian country of Uzbekistan, is a *United Nations World Heritage Site*. This means it has "cultural or physical significance." More than 70% of the town's population is Muslim, showcasing Islamic culture in centuries-old mosques, madrasahs, and mausoleums.

In 2012, Madina Samirov, along with her husband Aziz, and their daughter Shakhina, left Samarkand, the land they knew as home, for Queens, New York. Their hopes for new opportunities were similar to those of many others they met in the diverse backdrop of New York City.

The couple became pregnant with their second child soon after their move. "We were thrilled," says Madina. "The United States was a dream home, the ideal environment in which to raise children." Their elation quickly changed to fear when their doctor informed them that their baby had Down syndrome. Even worse, further tests and ultrasounds revealed deformed limbs and a serious heart condition.

Desperate for another opinion, the couple consulted a second doctor and then a third, but they only confirmed the initial report. Each doctor recommended that they abort the baby. Madina was in anguish and cried every day for a month. Finally, yielding to medical guidance, they scheduled a date for the abortion.

They moved forward with the plan, thinking they had no good alternatives. "Aziz, however, had an unusual dream that told him we shouldn't do it—that God had a special plan for the life developing inside my womb," Madina remembers, as if it were yesterday.

Just four days before the procedure was scheduled, Madina was in a park near their home, unsure of what to make of her husband's dream. She had gone there to escape the weight of what she was about to do, the turmoil of what it meant for them and their unborn child.

Inna Edelstein, an immigrant from Moscow was in the same park on the same day. As she and Madina started to talk and share the many things they had in common as immigrants, Inna began to share her Christian faith.

Inna's story reminded Madina of many years before, when she saw a man called Jesus in a dream. "What is the significance of Jesus?" she wondered as a young Muslim woman. She attempted to attend a home church meeting in search of an answer, but the congregation was closed due to government restrictions and her quest for an answer reached a dead-end.

Although Madina had wondered about Christianity ever since that dream, she had never heard about the gift of salvation through Jesus until this moment in the park. "What Inna told me made me know I had seen this Jesus in that dream," remembers Madina. "So right there on the spot I prayed to receive Him into my heart." Her husband arrived at the park a little while later and, after hearing what had just happened to Madina, he also surrendered his life to Jesus.

Two Muslims, turning to Christ in a park through the witness of a Jewish woman, on a Saturday afternoon in New York City—it seemed like a miracle all its own. However, it was just the beginning.

"Inna asked me about the grief and turmoil still apparent on my face. Tears began to flow. I told her about our plans to abort our pregnancy," Madina recalls. Then Inna shared her own testimony.

While living in Kazan, Russia, Inna had witnessed the miraculous healing of her son, Daniel, who had an incurable condition that eventually would kill him. They too had been desperate, until God completely healed Daniel. The healing led their entire Jewish family to call upon Jesus, the Messiah. As Inna shared this story, Madina was filled with hope that her baby in her womb could be healed. Together, they prayed out loud in the middle of the park, asking Jesus for this miracle.

Two days after meeting Inna, Madina went to her doctor for a checkup consisting of standard procedural tests. "Something had changed," Madina recalls in awe. Three doctors from three different departments of the clinic were stunned: the tests showed that Madina's baby did not have Down syndrome, deformed limbs, or a heart condition. Thinking they'd made a big mistake in their earlier diagnosis, the doctors apologized profusely. But Madina said to them, "This is not a mistake; it's a miracle! Jesus healed my baby!" Their miracle, Daniella Samirov, was born to the continued shock of the doctors. She was completely healthy, without any complications or deformities.

The Samirov family came to America for a better earthly life but they realized there was a higher aspiration—to know God, grow in faith, and meet the Great Physician of the Bible.

"What is the significance of Jesus?" The question, originally posed by a curious young girl living in a Muslim country, had finally been satisfied with the most powerful of answers.

Aziz, Madina, and their family are very happy living in New York City and continue sharing the gospel with friends and family in Central Asia. Since their miracle story, several of their family members have come to faith in Christ.

YADIRA AND GIOVANNY CAMPOS

Upper East Side, Manhattan

Yadira Campos couldn't explain the strange symptoms she was experiencing. Her husband, Giovanny, agreed it was time to see a doctor. After the checkup and tests, the doctor delivered the shocking news. "You have an advanced-stage cancer." Yadira, only in her 20's, was speechless. At a loss and wanting to comfort his wife, Giovanni told her, "Everything is going to be okay." The doctor turned to him and sternly warned, "Do *not* say that to her."

Giovanny could tell by his wife's face that she was petrified, and the doctor's words were making things worse. "We need to go somewhere else," he told her, as they abruptly left the room. Still in shock, Yadira asked, "Where are we going?" Giovanny had a plan and told her not to worry.

They grabbed a taxi from the Upper East Side to the midtown office of Every Nation Church, NYC. They arrived to find several of the pastors conducting their weekly staff meeting.

Giovanny pulled some of the pastors aside and told them what had just happened. Right there on the spot, everyone huddled together and prayed for the Campos. They prayed for healing, comfort, and wisdom, filling the room with their appeals to God while Giovanny and Yadira were sobbing.

Giovanny wasn't sure what he expected to find at the church when he hailed the cab earlier, but he sure didn't expect all of the pastors to be ready and available for an emergency prayer session. The fact that they were there and prayed so powerfully felt like nothing short of a miracle.

The Campos left and began to seek out another oncologist for a second opinion. After the appointment with this new doctor, they endured a two-week wait for the results.

"It was the most miserable two weeks of our lives," Giovanny remembers. "Every single day, I was down on my knees begging God for Yadira to be healed. Every time I looked at her I was trying not to break down and start crying." Giovanny did his best to keep calm as they were both fighting great hopelessness, weighed down by the news that her life would soon end.

Finally it was time to go back to for the second opinion. Braced for the worst, they could hardly believe their ears when the doctor said, "The tests show no cancer in your body. There is nothing cancerous present."

They were amazed and speechless. It all seemed too good to be true! They personally delivered the news to the pastors, who started shouting and praising God too. "It was such an extraordinary experience and, without doubt, a miracle," Giovanny recounts. He still marvels to this day.

Not long after, both Giovanny and his wife were baptized at the church offices, the same location where the pastors had prayed over them, dedicating their lives completely to Jesus Christ, their faithful Healer.

Although the miracle of the negative test was enough for the Campos, another chapter requiring divine intervention was about to unfold. Two years after Yadira's cancer-free diagnosis, she was told she could not have children. Their doctor, who was supposed to be one of the best in the city, ran a number of tests on Yadira. The results showed an estimated 10% possibility of ever getting pregnant.

"Well, 10% is not impossible," they decided to believe, and began a rigorous regimen of fertility injections. "It was a painful process, but my wife, driven by the hope of becoming a mother, kept her eyes on Jesus and the unwavering desire for a baby," Giovanny later recalled. When it came time to be tested to see if her chances of getting pregnant were improving, they found nothing changed. In fact, they met with another doctor who found their chances had dropped from 10% to 3%.

The doctor encouraged them to consider other options, like perhaps adoption. "Empowered by our 'mustard seed' of faith, we told him we were going to go for the 3%," Giovanny remembers. He also remembers the doctor's last words as they left his office that day: "Don't throw away more of your money."

They sought their pastors' prayers for yet another miracle and decided to go forward with a procedure, accompanied by faith-filled fervent petitions to heaven. In the second month of the procedure, the doctor told them surprising news. "Congratulations, you're going to be parents!"

"It was all like a surreal movie to me and I could barely believe it," says Giovanny. Eight months later, on October 31, 2009, the Campos were blessed with a healthy, beautiful baby girl. Their daughter is now almost 12 years old and thriving.

"The most devastating reports *can* change," reflects Giovanny. "I look at my daughter and my wife and am constantly reminded of the miracles He's done for us. And what He's done for us, He can also do for you."

Yadira and Giovanny Campos enjoy their lives, work, and family in Queens. They adore their miracle daughter and share their story often. Giovanny is honored to be the only contributor to Miracles in Manhattan who shares two stories in this book.

FARES

Hell's Kitchen, West Side Manhattan

It seemed to Fares that he was caught between two worlds his entire life. Born in Sweden of both Moroccan and Indian descent, he grew up in the Muslim nation of Morocco, where he attended a French International school. His mother, a Christian from India, raised her four sons as Muslims, obeying Islamic principles and practices. At night, though, she prayed with them on a regular basis.

Forced to keep Muslim laws, celebrate Ramadan, and not even mention what he was praying in secret, Fares was living among many contradictions that left him confused. Most times he chose to assimilate in order to be like those around him, fearful of standing out from his classmates.

While attending university in Paris, he was searching for even just one Christian, because he remembered a missionary couple he had met briefly years before. Their faith and kindness toward him, though brief, had left a lasting impression he could not shake. Painfully alone in the City of Lights, he found no Christians to befriend.

By now Fares was a young finance professional, excelling in business and pursuing a career that held much promise. At the same time, he was lonely and disheartened with his religious upbringing, and starting to explore views of radical religious groups who despised Western culture.

Every night he was reading about them online, intrigued by the passion they possessed, and their determination to recruit and rally others. A radical Imam paid him a visit, and explained what he could purportedly do to achieve higher status and eternal reward.

"My hate for Westerners grew, and I thought about killing everyone in my office," he remembers. Perhaps this would satisfy his longing to make an impact on the world, to find greater meaning and mission, he wondered? Then, seemingly out of nowhere, his company transferred him to New York City.

It was during this monumental move halfway across the world that Fares would not be able to resist his deep desire to know and understand Jesus—the One his mother had introduced him to on those nights when he was young and they would pray together.

On his very first Sunday in New York, he googled "NYC church," which led him to Every Nation Church, NYC. Upon visiting, Fares immediately appreciated the men's Bible study. "The guys were different somehow, which made me want to learn more," he recalls.

One of the men asked if he would like to join him in reading a chapter of the Bible every day, which he did. "After months of searching scripture, I still had doubts, says Fares. "I was still struggling, but was also gaining an understanding of the nature of Jesus and my identity as a son of God."

Adam Burt, a church pastor and a former NHL player, introduced Fares to Betty, a strong woman who lived passionately for God. This young man and older woman found they had much in common, including stories of Paris. Betty spent significant time pouring hope into Fares' weary, depressed soul. Betty, and her husband, Bill, had become his new "missionaries" whom Fares deeply admired.

The close-knit church community helped him start the process of defeating addictions and depression. Small steps led to significant changes, the kind that kept him going even when progress felt slow and insignificant. Looking back today, Fares defines it as the most important season of his life. Finally, he was not standing in the middle of conflicting worlds. He was linking arms with people who could help him find his true identity at last.

Fares was baptized at the same church he googled when he first came to New York. Today he works in East Africa, helping young men become entrepreneurs. His life has powerfully affected many others in the places he has lived, and he hasn't forgotten the community that led him here. "My dearest friends to this day are those I met when I first moved to NYC. We still stay in touch and support one another, because God is worth it!"

His road to change was, and still is, a process. "It did not happen in a day," he says. "Jesus became so very real as I turned to Him and confessed Him as Lord. It wasn't by being radical for religion, but through God's Spirit of peace that I received power to fight back against the strongholds in my life. Now I seek Him more every day. I don't have to be a slave to sin or depression anymore, because now I know who I am."

Fares is a global financial analyst working with banks, financial firms, and investment companies. His work focuses on helping the poor and disenfranchised in developing nations.

HEALTHCARE AND MEDICINE

Only a life lived in the service to others is worth living. Albert Einstein

During the COVID-19 crisis, every night at 7:00 in New York City for half a year, people came to their balconies or opened their windows to bang pots and blow whistles, recognizing the heroes of the city who were going into the danger zone to help save lives and heal the sick. The City actively cheered, prayed for, and saluted the front-liners from many professions, especially the nurses, doctors and hospital employees. As *The Washington Post* puts it, "The nightly ovation for hospital workers may be New York's greatest performance."

IN MY OWN WORDS

Dr. Michael Schaefer

The Bronx and Midtown Manhattan

I never aspired to live in New York City. Growing up in Michigan, I was simply moving to the city to be near Alyssa, the ambitious girl whom I met in college and fell in love with. When I was selected for an internal medicine residency program in the Bronx, I remember sitting on the edge of my bed and telling God, "If a career in New York is what You have planned for me, I'm all in." With Alyssa and the residency in sight, I made the move. Little did I know it was a move that would change the path of my life forever, allowing me to grow spiritually and be on the receiving end of two miracles.

Being raised in a Catholic family shaped my early years of religious faith. My father went to seminary for many years, hoping to become a priest before deciding it wasn't the right choice for him. I was baptized at a young age, and confirmed in the same Catholic Church we attended every Sunday.

Nothing would keep our family from attending Mass each week. Even during family vacations to Mexico or Florida, or traveling as a teenager to play competitive soccer, my devout parents made sure to find a Catholic Church in the area so we wouldn't miss Mass. I appreciated the discipline and foundation of God the Father and Christ his Son, yet though I knew *of* God, I didn't really *know* Him. Truthfully, I didn't even realize I *could* know Him.

During my time as a medical student, Alyssa and I were attending her church, Every Nation Church, NYC. It wasn't anything like what I was used to, but the music was lively and people raised their hands in worship. Accustomed to the formal hymns of Catholic mass, I didn't really know what it all meant and it felt foreign at first. Alyssa asked a question I found compelling, "If you can shout or cheer for a bunch of strangers throwing a ball down a field at a football game, can't we also cheer and wave our hands for our very Creator?"

Her question immediately clicked with me—an avid college football fan—but I wasn't sure if she was right. What I did know was it felt good to be in a place where people were genuinely happy and dedicated to God. After meeting a number of other church members, I thought, "Maybe there is something I've been missing in my faith journey all these years."

Growing in faith was a gradual process. It was a day-by-day decision to learn more, do more, and finally to feel the conviction that, yes, raising my hands while singing praises to God *was* an expression I liked! As my faith in God grew deeper, so did my relationship with Alyssa. On June 2, 2007, we got married. We have worked in New York City and lived in Hoboken for many years since.

Serving God wholeheartedly has brought deep meaning, not only to my faith journey and our marriage, but also in my work and calling. I work as a cardiologist based in midtown Manhattan. Every single day, I get to talk to patients and show them God's love, often at times when they're facing a serious diagnosis or uncertainties about their future health.

Sometimes I wonder, "Where else can they see and feel God's love in this great city?" So even when I'm having a less than perfect day, I can stop, look someone in their eyes and let them know I truly care, not only about their health but about their life and total well-being.

Alyssa and I have thought at times about leaving New York. It's not an easy place to live, raise a family, or be a Christian. Sometimes it feels like you're the only one who'd rather serve God than do whatever pleases you in the moment. Every temptation is alive and well here, and even seemingly harmless ones like fantastic restaurants or career opportunities can take your focus (and your wallet) off the right path.

Nevertheless, we made a commitment to both the city and the people of New York. Following Christ empowers that commitment to stay and serve in every way we can. Being part of our church community also grounded us. We have made many friends and been blessed with mentors who have been following Christ longer than we have. These relationships have sustained us and helped us grow, even during the toughest of times.

One such season began about 10 years ago. We had been married for a few years and were ready to start expanding our family with children, having no idea we would endure years of surgeries, treatments, and hopes deferred time and again. These were challenging times when we did not always feel like serving, but God gave us new hope and ways to "expand" His kingdom without children, such as teaching the young-married and engaged couples class at our church.

Our desire to become parents never wavered, and our "Connect Groups," (small groups from church that meet regularly to pray, study the Bible, and support one another), walked with us through the highs and lows, never giving up. Many times it felt like their faith was the only faith we had left.

Last year, in the middle of the COVID-19 pandemic we watched our dream of children become a reality, when God brought us newborn twins through adoption, something our Connect Group specifically prayed for, even though it looked impossible.

This miracle, and so many others, remind me of God's faithfulness in helping me find my calling—God's calling—to serve the people of this great city through medicine, while being a faithful husband, devoted father, and committed friend.

Dr. Michael Schaefer is a cardiologist based in Midtown Manhattan. His passion is sharing hope and faith with his patients and everyone he meets.

TIFFANY LENTZ

Tenth Avenue and 50th Street, West Side Manhattan

Dealing with bouts of intense fear, abandonment, and depression following an agonizing divorce, Tiffany Lentz decided to take a journey across the globe. *Maybe I'll discover who God really is or if there even* is *a God*, were her thoughts as she started packing. Tiffany was not quite sure of what she might discover, but one thing she did know for sure—*If God is who I've been told He is for the first 25 years of my life, I'm not interested.*

The years leading up to her travel plans were anything but photo-worthy. Shortly after college she married a man whose background matched hers. Tiffany's hopes were like any young bride, anticipating years of happily-ever-after.

Soon, however, unhealthy patterns emerged as she watched the culture of their mutual religious upbringing destroy her marriage, one "law" at a time. "Ours was a church culture built on works, hypocrisy, and fear," says Tiffany. "There was no place for a personal relationship with a God who is angry and withdrawn. His love and blessings only come if you make Him happy." Tiffany's marriage reflected the same.

After four years, she filed for divorce from her husband, and would have loved to do the same with her church. Their church leaders blamed her for her husband's abuse and asked her to leave the congregation. The shaming led her to a sad conclusion: "God is now angry at me for the sin of divorce."

Being shunned by church leaders wasn't the worst of her church problems. "I knew of multiple instances of child and spousal abuse 'to protect the name of Jesus,'" she recalls. Countless self-professed "Christian men" would treat women inside the church as weak, subservient, and incapable of meeting expectations. Horrified, she watched the same male abusers assume leadership positions, the very roles women were conveniently considered "unfit" to hold.

With shame now being handed to her with divorce papers, she was ready for a world adventure to forget about all of it, and perhaps, though unlikely, discover a higher, better way.

Over months and continents, Tiffany visited countless temples and monasteries, looking for God in the eyes of people she met, listening to their versions of truth, yet finding nothing that filled the void inside.

Returning from her travels, even more unsure of the future, her options were either New York City or Manchester, United Kingdom. "I visited Manchester but it didn't feel right," she remembers. Something seemed to be calling her to NYC for a fresh start.

As with most things up to this point, she felt God would be angry if she disobeyed. "I had no idea that the physical move I was making was really about a spiritual move of God on my behalf, a move that was going to change everything," she says.

A combination of guilt and the convenience of location led her to check out a new church shortly after arriving. "The large nondenominational church seemed like a place where I could ease my conscience and meet God's expectations at the same time," she recalls. As soon as she walked in, a girl introduced herself at the door and insisted they sit together on the front row of all places. Her self-consciousness disappeared quickly as the worship team began to sing.

This is the air I breathe. I'm lost without you. I'm desperate for you. These were beautiful and melodic words to Tiffany's ears, but she was struck by such a song and concept—that God actually seeks a personal relationship with His people? She was intrigued and undone in a way that surprised her.

Tiffany had never heard worship like this, and the wall she had put around her heart started to crack. "I was searching for God by traveling the world, battling depression and suicidal thoughts, succumbing to the lies of the enemy who told me I was not worth God's time. That search led me to one verse, of one song, on a single Sunday morning, one that was awakening my heart in a way nothing else had for seven years."

Tiffany's wounded heart continued to feel a pull to this congregation each week. The people were sincere and compassionate, the messages brought life to her weary mind and soul.

"I was encountering God deeply and personally for the first time in my life and wanted more," she says. The worship pastor befriended her with a gift of *The Message* translation of the Bible which she consumed as if she had never even heard of the Bible before. Ministries at the church such as Cleansing Stream helped her break away from the past, step out of her shame, and live as a free woman.

"I started to see Jesus outside of a church or denomination, outside of religious rules, separate from bigotry and anger. He was reaching me as Jesus the Son of God and embodiment of love." She quotes Romans 8:1 with certainty: "There is now no condemnation for those who are in Christ Jesus."

"People who knew me before my Christian conversion don't even recognize me as the same person anymore," Tiffany says with the confidence she wanted for so long. "I went on a search all over, only to discover it was God my Savior looking for me. *I* was found by *Him*, and He brought me home."

Tiffany Lentz manages the global non-profit arm of an international for-profit consultancy. Her mission is to bring better care to the poor and disenfranchised in developing countries through healthcare solutions, partnering with governments and local NGOs, using technology to make the world a better place.

DRS. ALLAN AND ALA MAY SANTIAGO

The Lamb's Theater, Times Square

They were gone. His wife and daughter had packed up, leaving the accomplished doctor alone. Years of pain and hurt had turned a tumultuous marriage into an official separation. Allan's family was broken, and there was no hope in getting them back. The worst part? He wasn't sure he wanted to.

Allan Santiago was raised in a large family in the Philippines, where he pursued medicine and became a distinguished doctor. In the early 1990s, he crossed paths with Ala May, who was becoming a medical doctor herself. "We were inseparable," Allan recalls.

Their love affair grew, and in 1998, Ala May was pregnant. This was not Allan's first child. He had his first child with another woman before meeting Ala May, a woman to whom he was still technically married. He was not particularly involved with his first child, so he focused on the life ahead of him with Ala May and his soon-to-be second child.

Allan's family of origin was large for reasons most would not care to admit. His grandmother had a second family, and so did eight of his nine siblings. Adultery and infidelity were rampant. "There was always a second family," he explained. Here Allan found himself inexplicably following the same pattern. He was starting a second family while still being legally tied to his first. Was there hope for a different pattern and life?

The couple decided to move to the States while Ala May was still pregnant and Allan's first marriage was yet to be annulled. They arrived in Honolulu with just $500.00 in their pocket. "We even had to split the money," Allan recounted because he could not afford to take Ala May with him to their final destination in New York City. Allan dropped her off at a relative's home and continued on alone. Something was pulling him to NYC and he wasn't exactly sure why.

He arrived in NYC and met his best friend who helped him settle down and find a job. He took a research assistant position at the Veteran Affairs hospital in Northport, New York, because applications for medical residencies were already closed at the time. He seized the opportunity, remembering a certain prayer from a pastor he knew before migrating: "When you get to the U.S., there will be only one door that is open and don't be afraid to go through it. God will be there." This carried him through a transition into U.S. medicine that to him was less than desirable.

Allan's title was technical, but the nature of the work was janitorial. "I was there to clean the mess of the molecular biologists who used the lab," he recalls. Hard work, frugality, and an immense amount of self-discipline paid off. By fall of that year, he was able to bring Ala May to join him. Allan obtained his medical residency in April of 1999, and soon thereafter married the mother of his second child, a little girl they named Abigail.

The couple settled in Long Island and continued in medicine, while raising their daughter together. Ala May established her own medical residency in New York City. They built successful careers in the city that never sleeps. The couple who came with only $500.00 to their name now were doing quite well.

In 2001, they began attending a church which started right after 9/11, Every Nation Church, NYC, where Abigail was the only child in the yet-to-be-started children's ministry. Allan and Ala May committed to attending and serving as they could, and they watched the church grow. It became a second family for them.

As the years passed, sadly, their marriage started to fray. Arguments became more frequent and heated. Time was compounding their wounds, not healing them. Ten years into their marriage, Allan and Ala May's relationship was broken, almost irreparably. At the apex of their marital conflict, Ala May separated from Allan, taking Abigail with her. Numerous friends and pastors had tried to intervene and counsel them. One piece of advice they wish would never be dispensed to anyone in marital stress came from a well-meaning advisor who plainly told Ala May to "Just divorce Allan." "It got that bad," Allan remembers.

One night while in a deep sleep, Allan awoke, "as if a bucket of cold water had been thrown at me," he recalls. He woke up instantly and heard someone tell him assertively, *Go back to Ala May.* He knew it was divine and resolved to do it immediately.

The couple pursued healing and reconciliation. Unearthing patterns of destruction was not easy. "The healing process took months, even years," Allan recalls. "There was deep hurt." They went through numerous sessions with different counselors to address the anguish and pain in their marriage, determined to find a path through.

Allan well understands the difficulty of couples who are struggling, and knows how it feels to be hopeless in that moment. When Ala May and Abigail left, he was already willing to let the marriage go because "I was full of pride," Allan says. "Once hurt comes in, it can really create a wound, one that grows worse over time. In these moments you and your spouse must decide what you want. The healing process is not easy. It takes good decision making. We did everything in our power to work on our relationship and break the generational patterns that had kept our families hurt and bound for years."

One good decision at a time turned into breakthroughs, small ones at first, then to a place of abiding peace, health and wholeness. "It took God's supernatural awakening for me to go back to Ala May," Alan remembers, with gratitude. "If I had not experienced that moment, I would not be telling you this story."

Nearly a decade ago, back in Hawaii for a leader's conference, Allan and Ala May asked their pastors Ron and Lynette to lead them in renewing their vows. There on the beach, with Abigail at their sides, they re-committed their lives to one another, knowing this time they were building on a solid foundation. They are still happily married, with three daughters, helping hundreds of others overcome hardships and live abundant lives. Dr. Ala May's favorite saying, "No shame, no blame, no guilt, no judgment," has encouraged others to give their marriage a second chance.

Drs. Allan and Ala May Santiago reside in Long Island where they practice medicine and specialize in infectious diseases and internal medicine. Ala May is a speaker and coach. Allan is a businessman and an entrepreneur. They have three daughters and are an inspiration to many.

MARJORIE BUFORD

Madison Square Garden

"God, this does not make sense!" Marjorie Buford, an associate real estate broker based in Harlem, lamented during prayer. Daily she was pouring anointing oil on herself—an ancient practice from the Israelites and Christians—because she felt impressed by God to do so, but had no idea why.

She obeyed nonetheless, for several months. Then, on Oct. 22, 2002, a car hit Marjorie and threw her into the air like a rag doll. "I had a broken leg, a broken shoulder, and my hip and spine were severely out of alignment," Marjorie recounts. She never had surgery—God protected her and over time, healed her.

This was not Marjorie's first near-death experience. Her life had been so full of peril, one might wonder how she made it through alive. She was just a baby when her stroller rolled down a hill, resulting in a serious head injury. She was hospitalized twice more as an infant due to severe asthma attacks. A few years later, her brother's friend put a gun to her head and pulled the trigger during a game of Russian roulette. A stranger tried to assault her with a brick. One time a stranger shot at her but she was protected. Marjorie confesses daily, "I am a daughter of the King."

Marjorie takes comfort in the knowledge that God's hand of protection has always covered her. "I now walk in the confidence that what the enemy meant for evil, God has turned around for my good," she says, quoting Genesis 50:20.

The fifth of eight children, Marjorie attended Catholic school where she began to notice she possessed the ability to know ahead of time what would happen. She learned to identify this as a prophetic gift, and it has been a part of her life many times over the years.

When her parents separated, she moved to the Bronx. After experiencing several personal traumatic betrayals between her early teens and mid-20s, Marjorie had a difficult time trusting people. "I became a person who saw an assassin in every bush," she recalls. "Trusting people was not an option for me." She became self-reliant, looking skeptically at everyone she met.

Such emotional posturing took a toll on her. It was Labor Day weekend 1996, when, at home by herself, Marjorie surrendered it all, and cried out to God. She'd made a mess out of her life that only He could fix. "Then my apartment was filled with the presence of God," Marjorie remembers. And for the first time since Catholic school, she heard the sound of God's voice: *If you* give *me your life, for the* rest *of your life, I will give you the desires of your heart.* From that moment on, her life was changed.

Marjorie got connected to Every Nation Church, NYC via a "divine appointment" in 2004, two years after her "thrown-in-the-air" accident. Watching Pastor Joel Osteen of Lakewood Church deliver a message about hope on television, she noticed a bulletin on the screen she had never seen before: "NYC Night of Hope at Madison Square Garden."

"My heart leapt," she said. "Somehow, some way, I knew I should be at that event, even though it was sold out." Marjorie prayed about it, and after several attempts to get a ticket, she attended one of Joel Osteen's book signing events in Midtown Manhattan with a letter of request. When she approached Joel, one of the assistants explained empathetically that he was not in a position to help. She lingered and silently asked God what to do. After some time, God impressed her to give the letter to *that* man, indicating one of the pastor's staff members, so she did.

Marjorie returned to her Washington Heights home around 5pm, walked inside and discovered a message on her answering machine. It said, "If Marjorie can get to the Plaza Hotel by 6 PM we have a ticket for her." Still recovering from her accident, she had to hobble all the way to the iconic NYC landmark hotel, but made it on time to get her ticket.

In a set-up that Marjorie knows now as one only God could orchestrate, the people seated next to her in the Madison Square Garden at the Night of Hope were Every Nation NYC pastors and leaders. After the event, Pastor Adam Burt walked up to her and said, "I've never seen anyone worship like you." He introduced Marjorie to the group and invited her to church. A few weeks later, she attended her first service and has been an integral part of the congregation ever since.

"I'm able to experience a 'whole life' as part of the Every Nation church family," she explains. "This is not a Sunday-only fellowship—I am speaking of doing *life* together, committing to the fellowship found in the book of Acts." Remarkably, she was healed, completely restored and has since run in several New York City Marathons.

Marjorie has used her spiritual gifts time and again as a leader in her church, praying for a "double portion" blessing that resulted in two sets of twins for Pastor Ron and his wife Lynette, and for another couple that struggled for over 10 years to have a baby. Her love for the needy is known around Manhattan where she has lived for decades.

Her busy real estate career took a turn into the field of medicine during the COVID-19 pandemic, where she now serves many patients through home healthcare, believing that the healing power of God that has touched her body time and again can be given to others needing healing as well.

Marjorie Buford works in three areas of work and calling: intercessory prayer for others; real estate to help people secure homes and change their environment; and healthcare to bring forth health, healing and wholeness.

SPORTS AND ENTERTAINMENT

If I can make it there I'll make it anywhere, it's up to you, New York, New York.
New York, New York, Frank Sinatra

New York City is host to 41 Broadway theaters, 11 major sports franchises, and an estimated 900 fashion companies. It has been famously called the, "city that never sleeps," and is for many the city where dreams are made and fulfilled.

IN MY OWN WORDS

Caitlin Rose

Starbucks, 43rd Street and Broadway

My life was dark, treacherous, and full of pain that almost pushed me over the edge. As a teenager I experienced many traumas and eventually this led to drug and alcohol abuse.

When I was scouted by a modeling agency and given the chance to pursue a lifelong dream, I seized it. Believing modeling was my way out, I moved to New York.

Most days felt like I was living my dream life. The world of modeling gave me access to the most prestigious nightclubs and the chance to meet some big names in fashion and entertainment. Sadly, I soon found out the people I admired most were empty, depressed, and—just like me—suffering from drug and alcohol abuse.

Shortly after my arrival in New York I had met Lara, a staff member of Every Nation Church, NYC. We hit it off and she became one of my only non-addicted friends. She would talk to me about Jesus and the church and would often invite me to special events. I'd make excuses and never show up. I did accept her offer to go to a Christian conference but slept through the whole thing. Despite this initial resistance, the church people impressed me. They all looked alive and vibrant, like they had a lightbulb glowing behind their eyes. I knew instinctively they were safe, loving, and filled with peace.

The influence of Lara and her friends at Every Nation began to affect me. It was during my first modeling trip overseas that I started to feel convicted of my sins and had an unfamiliar desire to become pure of heart. I didn't like who I was becoming. I hated the way I was behaving. I looked in the mirror only to see the person I never wanted to be. At one point, I broke down and cried out to God: "Lord, if you are real, then save me. There has to be more to life than this!"

In March 2003, I returned to New York City from abroad. Everything went wrong—*everything*. My agency told me I could no longer stay at the designated models' apartment. I had no money and nowhere to go. I didn't know what to do or whom I could ask for help, not even in my own family. "God, what do You want from me?" I looked at the sky as I prayed out loud. "What do I do?" Suddenly, there was a voice that told me, *Call Lara*. Of course. I always thought of Lara as a safe person, as someone I could trust.

I called her immediately. I could hardly speak when she answered and told me she just "happened" to be in a Bible study at a Starbucks in Times Square, only a few minutes away from where I was standing at that very moment.

I met her at the Starbucks at 43rd Street and Broadway and the instant I sat down, I felt the Holy Spirit for the first time. "Where have you been? I've been trying to call you," she said. I opened up and shared everything that was going on with me, even though I barely knew the other people with whom I was sitting. I felt safe and compelled to just empty my heart..

Lara and her friend, Brooklyn, asked me if I was willing to give my life to Jesus. I prayed the salvation prayer, but in the back of my mind I had doubts. I wanted God to prove himself to me—and he did. During that very moment I gave my life to the Lord, I instantly felt washed. I felt like Cinderella when she got her new dress. I walked out of that Starbucks a totally new woman. Everything felt different and looked brighter. I knew I was now one with Jesus.

The journey since has at times been rocky. There have been moments when I returned to the ways of the world. My battle with addiction was harder the second and third times around. However, every trial comes with its own life-changing lesson attached: I learned that because I wasn't being fully honest about the traumas I had experienced, the devil had a foothold in certain areas in my life.

It wasn't until I finally came clean about what I had been through that healing began to take place. Praise the Lord! He has delivered me, and I have been sober for nearly six years. I am now in ministry school, excited to see what God has planned, and eager for the chance to see the lives of others transformed through my story.

Being an active part of a church in New York helped lay the foundation of faith for me, especially through the "Biblical Foundations" course that I took during my first few years. That course, along with the words of faith that my mentors imparted have remained solid in my heart for the last eighteen years. Every journey is filled with twists and turns, but God never leaves or forsakes us. Every time we reach for Him, He is there, and we find that in reality, it's been Him reaching for us all along.

Caitlin Rose has been a professional model and actress for over 20 years. She is currently living in California attending a ministry school and being trained as a worship leader.

DEMARIO DAVIS

Florham Park, New Jersey

In 2012, Demario and Tamela Davis were driving to New York City after Demario was drafted by the New York Jets. They knew almost no one in what would be their new home town but felt excitement and expectation at this new season for their family.

As they drove, Demario silently prayed, asking the Lord to connect him to the right people. "Many look up to those of us in the spotlight, and I'm constantly aware of the need to lean into others who are tested, proven, and mature in their faith," he says. "I was praying for someone to stand with me over my life, character, and roles as father, husband, and friend."

The stats of so many pro athletes are widely reported. The narratives of those who "foul out," lose their marriages, or end up without a dime after retirement are sobering stories, often in the news. "I've always wanted a different outcome," says Demario, "one that pleases God and honors my family." He knew this prayer would take action on his part and not just hopeful faith.

Fortunately, his prayer was answered as soon as he met the Jets' team chaplain, Adam Burt. "Adam was the perfect mentor. As a pro athlete in the NHL for years, he knew the rigors, the lifestyle, and the pitfalls of being a pro athlete. My wife and I are fortunate we got to build a great relationship with him," recounts Demario.

Demario was invited to Adam's church, Every Nation Church, NYC, and began attending regularly at the New York City location as well as the location in New Jersey. With strong church support and a burgeoning relationship with Pastor Adam and Pastor Shino, another former pro football athlete on the church staff, Demario's relationship with God grew. "I didn't wait around—I instantly started connecting with church members, hearing great teaching of the gospel, and experiencing true worship. It was a wonderful place for my family to grow and be challenged."

Pastor Adam recognized Demario's desire to speak and share his story with others so the two traveled together to student campus conferences and places where they could serve, speak, and inspire others to live lives of purpose and grow in God.

"If I could use one word to define those years in my life it would be 'family,'" says Demario. "This family is something every person needs. It extends beyond the natural family and fills in the gaps, strengthening us where we are weak, and growing us beyond what we see for ourselves."

Through wins, losses, recognitions, and regrets, this community was on Demario's team for winning in life and relationships helping him cultivate a life mission that will continue even when a job or his career ends. Although these divine connections may not technically be called a miracle, they've helped set Demario's miracle of a life on the right path. "The Lord saved me and has kept me, something that still amazes me after all these years," he recalls. "The power of the gospel in the community of faith is the anchor for us all."

He sums it up by explaining, "No matter where you go, in the limelight or not, to have people praying for you, looking out for you, shepherding you, and speaking the word of God over you—that's priceless, and that's the real "win" on the playing field and in life."

Demario Davis, is an NFL linebacker who was originally drafted by the New York Jets and now plays for the New Orleans Saints. He was a first-team All-Pro in 2019, a second-team All-Pro in 2020, and received the Bart Starr Award in 2021. Demario is considered one of the most significant influencers in the NFL. He shares God's love in his city, at the border, and around the world. His wife, Tamela, is an extraordinary wife, mom, and Bible teacher.

GENELLE WILLANGER

The Lamb's Theater, Times Square

Genelle Willanger's life was glamorous, posh, and the epitome of luxury. A mega-successful model in New York City, her image could be seen on magazines everywhere.

Four times she graced the cover of *Maxim*, an international men's magazine, and also modeled for Abercrombie & Fitch, Prada, Valentino, Tommy Hilfiger, Nike, *Cosmopolitan*, and *Glamour*, among others. Genelle's acting career included major films such as *Something's Gotta Give* with Jack Nicholson and *The Devil Wears Prada* with Meryl Streep.

But what some might see as success was more like a prison for Genelle. Her life was, as she describes, "empty and meaningless." She struggled with drugs, alcohol, and bad relationships that led to sexual and physical abuse. "I felt alone in the modeling world," she says. "The glamour did not live up to its reputation."

Genelle could trace her problems back to middle school, where she was bullied and an outcast, leaving her starving for affection. Her home life with a distant father was no haven—she was kicked out at the age of 18. "Lost in a world of hopelessness, feeling like I had nowhere to go, I moved to New York City with my drug-dealer boyfriend to pursue modeling." When she came across a Joyce Meyer book, *Be Anxious for Nothing*, the first seeds of God's love were planted with a glimmer of hope. "Some things began to change," Genelle said. "However, there were still many more things I needed to overcome."

In 2004, a classmate at an acting school in Manhattan invited her to a prayer meeting at the Lamb's Theatre. "Hungry for God, I gladly accepted," she recalls. "That night I saw people passionately praying in unity. I longed for what they had." When she asked for prayer, everyone turned and prayed for her. "I immediately felt a holy fire touch my body and began to feel the power and love of God's Spirit," she remembers. Genelle started bringing her friends to this church—Every Nation Church, NYC—and began attending herself on a regular basis. The pull of her old ways was hard to resist though, and a few months later she started doing drugs again with her ex-boyfriend.

"I recognized the fierce battle being waged inside my heart," she says. High on drugs, she returned to the prayer meeting she had discovered only months before, desperate, surrendering to God, pleading for help. Like a family committed to one of their own, the church staff, leaders, and members all sprang into action.

At Genelle's request, they directly intervened, moving her into an apartment right above the Lamb's Theater. Her new roommates were strong Christian women who loved her and led her as she took steps out of her destructive patterns and relationships. Her new church family also nursed her back to physical health. "It was a shelter in the storm during the darkest night of my soul," Genelle says. "It was my true home where I was baptized in water and the Spirit, learned the Bible, and learned who God was—as well as who *I* was *in* Him." For the first time in her life, she felt loved.

Throughout that time of restoration, Genelle's modeling and acting career was accelerating. However, most of her assignments were degrading and didn't match this new person she was becoming. "I no longer wanted to do 'sexy' modeling, but had no idea how to change my perceived image."

When she decided to meet with her agents to set new boundaries, she thought they would drop her. "However, before I could even say anything, they announced they were going to change my image to a more wholesome look!" Genelle was awed by God's tangible intervention—nothing less than a miracle once again.

From that season forward, Genelle's life has been a testament to God's power and faithfulness. She met her husband Erik, also a model, in what became for both of them a transformative, committed church community, one they still value today.

"My heart is honored by the lifelong friendships and memories from that time in my life—a time which was the foundation of my walk with God. I will always be grateful for the many people who, right by my side, also found hope and love in a broken city."

Genelle Willanger is an actor, model, artist, wife to Erik, and mother of three. Her passion is helping creatives and artists encounter God through artistic expression. She graduated from ministry school and now serves as a family pastor.

RYAN AND TIFFANY NEILL

Rutgers University

An extraordinary student athlete, Ryan Neill played football for Rutgers University from 2001 to 2005. He was a success on campus and the football field, garnering the attention of many NFL teams. Ryan's life was looking up on all levels. He received numerous recognitions and awards from *Sports Illustrated*, the Academic All-American choice award, and others, but something he would describe as "even more significant" was just about to happen.

One day after practice, the Rutgers football coach invited the team to an event in New York City called "The Night of Champions" at the Lamb's Theater in Times Square. The coach heard about the event from Shino Prater, a former Penn State and NFL player, who asked the coach to consider bringing his team.

"The opportunity sounded really cool, especially coming from former NFL players with incredible careers," remembers Ryan. "It was exactly what I wanted for my future." So he and his teammates decided to go and headed to the Lamb's Theater.

Ryan didn't know quite what to expect when he arrived that evening. His Christian upbringing had left him with no real deep understanding or personal connection with God. When he heard the athletes share their stories, however, he knew there was something different about them. “They were more than just professional athletes; they spoke boldly about Jesus, which I found impressive and convicting.”

As Ryan was walking out of the theater that night, Shino grabbed the big lineman and said, "Hey, why don’t you guys come have a meal with us?" Ryan and his teammate, Dan, jumped at the offer.

Hearing those athletes and then having dinner afterwards, started something new in Ryan’s heart that night. In the weeks that followed he didn’t want to miss one service at Every Nation Church, NYC, the church that sponsored “The Night of Champions.” Other teammates started attending with him too. Soon they were hosting a Bible study for athletes that met on campus at Rutgers.

“Spiritually and psychologically, all of this changed my trajectory,” Ryan recalls. “From the Night of Champions forward, I started seeing my athletic aspirations through a new lens. I still wanted to succeed but for different reasons now. For years, everything had been about my talents, my skills, how I was playing, the coaches and fans who did or didn’t know my name. Now there was another name that mattered more to me, the One who was responsible for any of the awards or recognitions. I was hungry to grow more and know more.”

About that time, Tiffany Klebez started participating in the Bible study at Rutgers and was soon attending Sunday night services at the Lamb’s as well. In her words, “I grew up with no background in faith or religion. It was all new to me. I knew nothing about Jesus, except for the art paintings I studied as an art history major. But now, thanks to Ryan’s Bible study, I longed to know more.”

Tiffany recounts, “This was an incredible season for so many of us on the Rutger’s campus. I started relating to God as the father I’d never known.. I grew up in a divorced home where my dad was ‘in and out.’ Unlike my home life, I was now connecting with God and accepting His unconditional love. Through the church and Bible studies, I discovered I could have a safe and secure relationship far greater than my relationships with anyone else."

Ryan adds, "As we were getting to know God, we naturally wanted Him to be known to our friends. We were introducing many athletes to Christ and they were strengthened, joyful, and changed," Ryan remembers.

Ryan and Tiffany spent two years dating and riding the train from Rutgers to Times Square each week. Pastor Adam Burt officiated their wedding in 2005. Adam and his wife Susan helped Ryan and Tiffany through premarital counseling and have stayed close to them through the highlights and challenges of their lives in the years since.

After graduating from Rutgers, Ryan and Tiffany headed to Buffalo, New York, where he played for the Bills, before moving on to the Rams, and then the Chargers in 2010. Through it all, they felt God guiding their every step, and walking with them through each new season..

When Ryan retired from the NFL, he and Tiffany came back to Morris County, New Jersey to pursue careers in sales. They also actively serving the Every Nation Church, New Jersey congregation, just up the road from Rutgers where it all began.

"Perhaps the greatest miracle for me personally," Ryan says, "is how God found me, an athlete at Rutgers, then led me into New York City to hear the gospel, and then used me to impact so many lives for Jesus. I'm humbled and truly grateful that all those awards I once attributed to my own talents became secondary to the power of God to save someone's life."

Ryan and Tiffany Neill reside in Long Valley, NJ, with their children Alyssa and Brody. Ryan, a former NFL player, now works for Stryker Corporation as a sales leader. Tiffany is an owner of Couture Traders, LLC.

HOLLY ROSER

Upper East Side Manhattan

Holly Roser was clear about what she wanted to do in New York City, and it didn't involve going to church. "I had plans to expand my wellness business, make money, and become well known. That was it."

Everything started out according to plan for Holly when she moved to New York in 2011. She spent every waking moment working with her high-profile NYC clients, helping them in her fitness and nutrition business, enjoying appearances on shows like Dr. Oz. If she wasn't working, she was partying. "I was trying to fill the void in my heart." Holly vividly recalls. She also fell into a relationship with Allen, whom she thought cared for her. Still, the void she felt grew deeper and deeper.

Years earlier, back home in Silicon Valley, a friend invited her to a church—at least twenty times over nine months! Holly finally relented and drove almost an hour one-way to attend the service, only to be disappointed. "Nothing happened. My brain was completely lost in the mix, wondering how I ended up there," Holly said. However, that experience planted a seed. She began watching Joel Osteen on TV who, at the end of every message, encourages viewers to look for a local church.

Now years later, working like crazy in New York City, she clicked on the TV one evening and saw a familiar face: Joel Osteen. Though she had glossed over his final admonition countless times in the past, the words, *Go to our website and find your Bible-based local church* now jumped out at her from the bottom of the screen. "Clicking that button, far from family or friends in a new city, I was directed to Every Nation Church, NYC. I decided to attend with a friend that week."

Holly attended and immediately got a positive impression. "A church that meets in a movie theater. I can do this; this is cool," she thought. Holly's experience felt new this time. She cried the entire service without understanding why. "I looked over at my friend, and she, too, felt something in the room," Holly remembers.

Afterwards she talked to one of the pastors, Pastor George Gregory, who prayed with her, and she felt different. "He was bold enough to ask me if I had a relationship with God," Holly recalls. "I told him I didn't pray and didn't read the Bible." The pastor offered to pray with her, and she was grateful when he said, "I'm not here to push you but guide you on your spiritual walk with God." They prayed together and Holly knew something inside of her had changed.

As she headed back to 73rd Street on the bus, she wrote a prayer in her note-taking app, addressing something that had been pressing on her heart: "God, if my boyfriend Allen is the one for me, please make it apparent and obvious. Give me a sign to know that he is—or isn't—the one." Within an hour, she received a phone call from a woman who said she had received a call from Holly's phone number. "Do you know who a man named Allen is?" the woman asked, and began sharing news about Allen.

"That call made me sick to my stomach," Holly remembers. "Allen cheated on me while I was away at the funeral of my aunt—the only woman who ever helped me and believed in me," Holly said. "Outside of a miracle, I still don't know how that woman had my phone number that afternoon. But I knew it was God answering my prayer and showing me his power to lead and guide."

Two months after that supernatural experience on the Upper East Side, Holly was baptized, calling it the best day of her life. It was that moment when she was freed from everything the world had offered her but never granted. She found peace instead of turmoil, direction instead of despair.

Today, Holly is married to Jonathan whom she describes as "my true man of God." Together they are starting a church in Silicon Valley. "How cool is that?" Holly says. "God uses the broken, the lost, and the hurting to help others in similar situations. I left the life of partying and drinking for good, God found me in my wandering and wondering, and I've never looked back."

Holly Roser is a celebrity fitness personality and trainer in Silicon Valley and New York City. Featured on the Dr. Oz Show, CNN, The Washington Post, and Self and Shape magazines, Holly brings fitness, nutrition, and wellness to others.

CLARK

Theater District, Midtown Manhattan

Clark was only five years old when he first thought: "One day I'm going to live in New York City." To him, it was more than just a fantasy; he believed it would really happen. Years later, the dream would indeed happen but then morph into a nightmare. Mercifully, that is not where Clark's story ends.

Clark was an artistic child with a penchant for fashion, design, and all that was aesthetic. "My family didn't really 'get me,'" he remembers. As he grew older, he was bullied and taken advantage of before he was even a teen. Racked with pain and serious abuse, this stole from him any chance he had for a healthy, nurturing childhood.

One night, Clark's cousins, who had been having deep spiritual experiences, invited him to pray with them. He was 15 years old. "As we knelt at the side of the bed," Clark recounts, "a wind began to blow through the window, and the words came to me, 'Behold, I stand at the door and knock.'" That hot summer evening Clark accepted Jesus into his heart and was baptized in a bathtub at his cousin's house. The decision was real and sincere, but he still felt trapped and confused, burying the pain and sadness from his abuse.

Years passed. Clark graduated from Ohio State University and said goodbye to his fraternity brothers to pursue his dream of living in New

York City. He was ambitious, spurred on by the famous lyrics sung by Frank Sinatra,

"I want to wake up in a city that never sleeps,
and find I'm king of the hill, top of the heap!"

Clark's first job was at the iconic Radio City Music Hall. He excelled at his job and worked his way up. Years later he transitioned to work at *TV Guide* and then NewsCorp. Making six figures by now and married, he was rubbing shoulders with elites like Mikhail Gorbachev, Henry Kissinger, and Rupert Murdoch. He had certainly achieved "king of the hill" status. Even so, the nagging, toxic secret about what had happened to him as a young boy was chipping away at his mental, emotional and spiritual health. He felt helpless in confronting the hidden torment and unrelenting pain.

Around 2001, shortly after the events of 9/11, Clark began experimenting with crystal meth. "During this time, I was wrestling with two belief systems," Clark recalls. "The first was healthy and encouraging: I am made in the image of God and am worthy for who I am, not what I do. The other was poisonous: I am a fake. My career is based on fraud. If only I could become as good as all the others."

Clark caved in to the pressure and the guilt. His marriage was falling apart and his drug habit had drained his accounts. As his world was crumbling, a friend invited him to church and he accepted. The church was Every Nation Church, NYC.

He visited once and two weeks later returned after a week-long meth binge. The message strongly moved him and after the service ended, Clark approached the stage to ask a pastor for prayer. Afterward, Clark gave Pastor Adam Burt his business card.

That night on his way home, Adam left his wallet in a taxicab. The cab driver found it and fortunately did the right thing by trying to return it. The only phone number in Adam's wallet, however, was Clark's. Clark's contact with Adam led to a returned wallet and their first one-on-one meeting. Clark took it all as a divine connection, since to him his very survival seemed to be at stake. As the years went on, Adam became a friend and counselor. Clark jokes, "I always say if that wallet had not been lost, I might never have been found." Sadly, his next 10 years got even darker. He was in an all-consuming battle with crystal meth. Although Pastor Adam and others were helping, he had many relapses due to his own guilt, shame, and struggles. One particular setback almost cost his life.

"I did so much meth that I walked onto a subway platform while hallucinating and was invited down onto the subway tracks by what I'm convinced was a demon," Clark vividly recalls.

While walking to the far end of the platform and approaching the narrow steps leading onto the tracks, he clearly remembers, "Two hands grabbed me and pushed me to the ground between the trains coming and going. I was unable to move for the entire night, laid out amidst trash, rats, and feces. Strangely, not one rat bit me. The two hands I never saw restrained me from 9 pm until the next morning. Covered in grime and dripping with shame, I got up and walked off, ascending the same narrow steps I had descended the previous night."

The experience shook him and he tried even harder to stay on the right path but relapsed again almost six months later. He recalls, "Not long after I injected the drug this time, I heard horrifying screams and the words, "Outer darkness!" echoing in loud, eerie voices. I heard shrill cries and was terrified. I sensed these were cries from hell. My rebellion, pride, and sexual perversion all lay before me."

A few hours later, exhausted and afraid, Clark prayed tearfully, "My God, I repent!" His prayers were those of deep confession. "I knew this was my last chance and thought, 'Is this what it takes to save my life—hearing hell itself?'"

Since that moment, Clark has seen many more valleys and mountaintops, but he knows what it takes to live the life God intends: "Pray and pray. Test everything because we live in very dark days. Keep your eyes on God's eternal rewards. Read the Bible and confess your sins to one another. Pick yourself up and stay in church. God will show you the way."

Countless leaders in his community have helped Clark throughout the years. They persevered even when he pushed away the very people who were doing their best to save his life. He wasn't always appreciative of their efforts and often lashed out.

"I am incredibly indebted to them," Clark says with gratitude. "Looking back now, it's clear that they were embodying the hands and heart of Jesus, the only One who can set a man finally, totally free."

Clark lives in New York City, working in production, live events, and design. He is 11 years sober and continues to overcome.

LAWRENCE CHERRY

Park Slope, Brooklyn

Models and actors by the thousands fill the studios and streets of New York City. On Broadway, television, films, and billboards, their faces grace covers and their voices thrill audiences, day and night—that is, until the pandemic of COVID-19 hit Manhattan and its surrounding boroughs. Now the streets are empty, as are the bank accounts of many in the entertainment industry.

Lawrence Cherry was one of them. For 40 years he has lived and worked in the entertainment capital of the world, doing print advertisements in between jobs as an actor on some of the most popular television shows and films. He has seen it all and done it all in his industry. Even so, like the rest of the world, the pandemic took him by surprise.

"Before everything dried up, I was featured on a print advertisement for a popular eye medication," Lawrence remembers. "It's a medicine used for patients coming out of eye surgeries. I never endured any sort of eye issues but a year or so before, my doctor discovered cataracts." Fortunately, the doctor said the cataracts were "small and insignificant." Regular follow up exams kept showing the same. Life went on and jobs came in, and Lawrence forgot about the eye medicine and the cataracts.

Fast forward to 2020, when this industry veteran was not working. At the same time, the cataracts were significantly impeding his vision and he had no way of paying the several thousand dollars per eye that it would cost to get them removed. He fully expected his insurance to cover the procedure, until he learned that insurance companies labeled these "invasive cataract surgeries" as simply "cosmetic." They refused to pay all but the most minimal costs.

"As a lifetime actor," Lawrence says, "I *know* 'feast or famine.' In the middle of the pandemic, we all knew it at a whole new level. I also know the power of prayer, and have seen it bring miracle after miracle over the course of my life and career. Facing this new challenge was a very good time to pray!"

Lawrence and his wife, Yelena, were active in their church, often joining the 6 a.m. daily prayer calls. Sometimes it was a small group on the line, other times it was larger, as callers prayed for the church, the city, and individual prayer needs of those on the calls.

"We all prayed, and my wife and I put it in the hands of the Lord, just like we've done a hundred times before," Lawrence recalls. "What happened next is nothing short of a miracle," he says with conviction. "Neither my wife nor I can attribute it to anything else."

The post-op cataract-medicine ad he had appeared in years before, suddenly ran again, meaning a significant payment for Lawrence at the precise time his eyes needed surgery. "A seemingly out-of-the-blue call from my agent was making both eye procedures possible," he marvels. "And the fact that this same medicine became my own recovery medication after surgery was not lost on me!"

Beyond any possible coincidence, Lawrence knew his prayers were heard and answered. So many unrelated factors came together with precision and timing for his eyes *and* his finances. "God literally brought me one more 'in-your-face' miracle," Lawrence says, smiling.

"Without getting the least bit preachy," he concludes, in the deep smooth voice that has earned him roles for years, "I can say we have a

God in heaven who answers prayer. He knows what we need and when we need it. I've *seen* Him do it for me."

Lawrence Cherry has been an actor, model, and voice actor for four decades, producing, creating and starring in movies and shows including The Maltese Holiday, FBI Most Wanted, *and* Ramsey. *His great passions are his wife Yelena, their family, art, his home in Brooklyn, cooking, and his famous maple walnut banana pudding.*

LYNNE KOPLITZ

Greenwich Village, Lower Manhattan

It all started on an airplane, when a married couple that always sits together on flights somehow got separated. The husband was now seated on the aisle seat with an attractive woman in the middle seat beside him. She was hung-over, sucking on a lollipop, and as the plane took off, they struck up a conversation.

The woman, Lynne Koplitz, a well-known stand-up comedian based in New York City, had no problem talking to strangers. When the man, Ron Lewis, a pastor from NYC, pulled out his Bible to read during the flight, Lynne thought, "Are you kidding me, God? Is this what I get for drinking last night? You put me next to a Bible thumper!" Before long she was unraveling her entire life story to her newfound friend.

Prior to the flight, Ron and his wife had just left the bedside of his dying mother in Greensboro, NC. They were torn leaving her, but she urged them to go since Ron's sister was now at her side. Next thing they knew they were waiting for hours on the tarmac before takeoff, along with Lynne and the other passengers.

As Lynne began talking to Ron, he sensed that what seemed random and ill-timed was actually a divine appointment. He kept listening as Lynne unfolded personal details.

"My jokes are good and my mouth is bad," she began. "Growing up in Sarasota, Florida, my mom asked me what I wanted for my seventh birthday. I knew immediately—a Bible. This energetic little girl felt God speaking to her through the stories. She could feel Jesus, His gentleness so near, especially in this season when her parents were divorcing.

"One night when I was 12, my mom was on a date and I was alone in our scary apartment. I said, 'God, if You're here, I will believe You forever if You just light up this room right now.'" Just moments later her mom walked in, then a car pulled up with its lights flooding through the window in her room. "From that point on, I knew Jesus was my friend. When my single mom didn't have time to explain things to me, He did."

The plane took off by now and the flight to NYC was half over, though neither Ron nor Lynne noticed. They were deep in conversation and Lynne was deep into her own memories and soul. By this time, her hangover was gone.

"I came to realize that my life started unraveling the day I lost my virginity at age 19," she continued. "Really?" said Ron, "See my wife Lynette, seated over there by the window across the aisle? She was a virgin when we married at 42, maybe she can encourage you!" Ron said, cautiously laughing.

"Wait, what's her name? My name is Lynette—I just go by Lynne! And only God could send me a pastor on a plane with a virgin wife Lynette to answer my prayer!" Lynne exclaimed. No one but she and God knew she that she had been praying for months to talk to a pastor.

"I lost a lot of my power when I lost my virginity," she continued. "I've looked for healthy relationships for years since, with most ending in heartbreaks and abuse."

The string of relationships hadn't been all a loss, however. Lynne turned her pain into humor, as most comics do, on stages from Las Vegas to Hartford, Connecticut. Working with the likes of Joan Rivers, Jenny McCarthy, and Louis CK, she has earned laughs and an up-and-down salary from comedy clubs and other venues, large and small.

The flight landed. Ron, Lynette, and Lynne walked to the baggage claim together. They exchanged phone numbers, and Lynne joined them for church weeks later. It was something she would do over the next 15 years when her work and travel schedule permitted.

Lynne would have many more stories and moments when she needed a pastor. "You two always call me at just the right time," she often tells Ron and Lynette. One of her stories they all remember well.

"I was down to $50 in my bank account, doing a gig in the worst part of New Jersey at a yoga studio," Lynne recounts. "So I'm doing this one for just $200, and a blind man is heckling me. I get in a car heading home and I'm saying, 'God, I know You didn't bring me this far to drop me on my head, but must You let me dangle here this long?'"

An hour later, Lynne noticed an unusual text message on her phone from a number she didn't recognize. The man was asking if she could open for one of the most famous names in comedy, at Madison Square Garden. "Wait, what? I must be reading this wrong," she thought. The text ended with, "Let me know if you can do it. It's in three days."

At this point Lynne was stunned, thinking, "I just turned 50. Who has an opportunity like this at 50, at a time I'm thinking of giving up comedy all together? I have $50 dollars in the bank, plus the $200 I just made at the yoga studio."

Lynne didn't even blink; she said yes. The show was a hit. She was paid very well, and significant new doors have opened up since then.

"Comedy is the gift God has given me," she says. "So often I'm walking on stage saying, 'Jesus, hold my hand! I'm terrified.' Sometimes I feel so bad because I may not be bringing enough glory to God in my routines. But what Ron tells me helps when he says, "You're a backdoor evangelist, Lynne. Just listen to God, you'll know what to do."

Lynne has many stories, some funny, others painful. To her, all of them represent God's faithfulness and grace. "Everything we've ever wanted is waiting for us, just like a wrapped gift in a closet," she believes. "Maybe we aren't ready for it yet, but it's in there, and God is there, waiting for just the right time. He knows exactly how to get it to us, no matter where we are—even on an airplane."

Lynne Koplitz is a stand-up comedian and actress, appearing at Madison Square Garden, on many Comedy Central specials, NBC, Food Network, Sony Pictures and more. In 2009, she co-hosted the inaugural broadcast of StarTalk radio with astrophysicist Neil deGrasse Tyson. In 2017, she released her first Netflix special, titled Hormonal Beast, dedicating it to her friend Joan Rivers. She lives in the Greenwich Village neighborhood of Manhattan with her dog Gertie.

IN MY OWN WORDS

Adam Burt

New York City

The 1987 NHL entry draft held in my hometown of Detroit was a moment I will never forget. My selection in the second round by the Hartford Whalers—who later became the Carolina Hurricanes—meant my life as a professional hockey player had begun.

My career in the game I loved would span 14 seasons with so many great moments and memories. I planned to go right into broadcasting when my playing days were over. But that didn't happen.

Have you ever heard the saying, "If you want to make God laugh, tell Him your plans?" In 2001, just months before the events of 9/11, I laced up my skates to battle the NY Rangers at Madison Square Garden. It would be the last hockey game I'd ever play. My first profession was about to finish just a few blocks away from where my second one would begin, though I had no idea at the time.

My wife, Susan, and I sensed a call from God to join Ron Lewis, who reached out to me when I first started playing for the Hurricanes in Raleigh years before. Ron shared with us what was happening in New York City out of the ashes of 9/11 and compelled us to join the ministry. Deciding to follow this call, we sold everything and with our two young daughters, moved from Austin to Manhattan, where I became a pastor on staff at Every Nation Church, NYC. God must have laughed.

While the city was still recovering, I too was recovering from the shock that a career in hockey had now changed into a vocation I barely understood: full time ministry. Voices in my head were often clamoring, "What are you doing? Are you crazy?" Looking back now, I can see God was directing us all along.

An evangelist rolled through one of our church services, and Ron had him pray over me. The man stopped in the middle of his prayer and declared, "You will reach thousands of athletes for Christ." Frankly, I was unimpressed and just forgot about it until a week later, when one of the NY Jets players showed up at our Westside service. He approached me and said, "You should be our team chaplain." I thought he was joking, but apparently not, as I've been the team's chaplain now for 14 years. True to the words of that evangelist, God has used my simple "yes" to ministry as a means of impacting thousands of athletes.

Over the years, I have marveled at the brokenness in NYC. I know pain quite well with injuries on the ice: 500 stitches, nearly 50 screws and 20 plates implanted, a knee reconstruction, staph infections laying me out for weeks, and five back surgeries that eventually ended my career. Hockey can take its toll on a body, but living in a broken world takes its toll on a life.

As a minister, I've had a ringside seat in that arena of life, where God touches the most diverse and often unlikely people with miracles. Hundreds of stories later, two come to mind.

There was a famous opera singer at the iconic Metropolitan Opera who seemed to have it all, yet inside was hurting as she struggled in her marriage on the verge of divorce. Her quest for answers led her to one of our services, and as she listened each week, the pieces began to fall into place. I still remember the day she excitedly pulled me aside and displayed her wedding ring she had started wearing again. God, the great physician, healed this marriage.

Then there was the outlaw biker-gang leader who, having been on the wrong side of a knife fight, was quickly bleeding out as he made his way to the hospital. After hours of surgery and near death, he began to take inventory of his life. As God would have it, he met a woman who invited him to one of our services. He was hoping for a date, but got something greater: an encounter with God. For the first time in his life he had peace—complete peace and no fear. This man who once dealt in violence, sex, and drugs was now bringing people to church, giving to the poor, and sharing the gospel with everyone.

Answering the call of God to move to New York was probably the most terrifying decision I've ever made in my life, yet also the most satisfying. Watching so many miracles in Manhattan, in New Jersey, and all over our region, has been more rewarding than all the wealth I've ever had.

Here's my favorite way to compare it. During the 2000 NHL playoffs I was playing for the Philadelphia Flyers as we battled our in-state rival, the Pittsburgh Penguins. The game would prove to be the longest hockey game of all time. It started at 7 p.m. and finally finished at 3:30 a.m. We played for eight-and-a-half periods. That is almost three complete games. In the wee hours of the morning, we scored to win the game and eventually the series.

Sitting there in my sweat-soaked equipment, totally exhausted and spent, I felt this deep soul satisfaction. Looking into the eyes of my teammates we knew we'd given our all for one another, and the win was deeply gratifying.

In my nearly 20 years in New York City as a minister of the gospel, I have had a similar feeling, a deep soul satisfaction of pouring out life with others to watch Jesus Christ save people. In the end, we win this one too. But this win doesn't stop at eight-and-a-half periods. A life changed by Him lasts forever.

Adam Burt is a former NHL hockey player, current Pastor of Every Nation Church, New Jersey and the Chaplain of the New York Jets football team. He's happily married to his wife, Susan, and the proud father of two daughters, Cassandra and Elizabeth. His love of his dogs is notorious.

AFTERWORD

Dr. Rice Broocks

KEEP SPREADING THE NEWS

My Manhattan miracle began in Nashville, Tennessee, on 9/11/01. Sitting in my living room watching the events of that day unfold, I had a strong sense I needed to drive to New York City. As a minister, I felt compelled to do *something*, and not just watch the images on TV of the heartbreaking stories while sitting in the safety and comfort of my own home.

Our congregation held a prayer meeting the next night, and afterward, that same evening, a small group of us set out for the drive to New York. I had called my lifetime friend, Ron Lewis in Cary, North Carolina, and asked him to meet me in Manhattan on 9/13.

For the next few days walking the streets of the city, we talked to scores of people and felt the enormous despair that hovered like a cloud. Ron and I decided to work together to launch a ministry focused on people. Within a month, I flew in every Sunday afternoon, along with my associate, Pastor Tim Johnson, joining Ron who eventually felt the calling to become the senior pastor and would lead the new congregation forward.

My involvement in helping begin this church now known as Every Nation Church, NYC has been one of the great honors of my life. From the start, the church has had a clear sense of purpose to "start spreading the news" that Jesus Christ is the healer of the broken-hearted and the hope of the nations of the world. Though the issues facing the city, the nation, and the world were—and still are—daunting and complex, the Gospel remains the guiding light through these difficult times. The stories from this book are living proof of how true this is.

The message I want to leave with you is to *keep spreading the news of this Gospel* that brings hope and salvation for all people. And what is this Gospel?

It is the good news that God became man in Jesus Christ. He lived the life we should have lived and died the death we should have died...in our place. Three days later He rose from the dead, proving He is the Son of God. He offers the gift of salvation and forgiveness of sins to everyone who repents (turns) and believes in Him.

Here is what this means for you...

God became man in Jesus Christ: The Creator of the Universe entered His own creation as a human. Therefore, He understands our pain, sorrows, and needs.

He lived the life we should have lived: Jesus lived a morally perfect life on earth. All the major religions honor Christ as an exemplary moral teacher, yet none of the leaders of those religions claimed perfection like He did.

He died the death we should have died...in our place: There is a cost for breaking the laws of any nation. How much more for breaking the laws of God? Christ suffered the torturous death of a public Roman crucifixion on behalf of the sins of the world and fulfilled God's demand for atonement.

Three days later, He rose from the dead, proving He is the Son of God: The resurrection of Christ from the dead happened in history. This is the foundation of the Christian faith and verification that our faith is based on evidence and eyewitnesses, not wishful thinking.

He offers the gift of salvation and forgiveness of sins: Imagine having a debt you can never pay, suddenly forgiven. The joy of the burden of our sins being canceled is what Christ offers us. The gift of salvation means we can be made whole, regardless of how broken we are, and then receive eternal life.

For everyone who repents and believes in Him: To repent means to turn away from darkness and unbelief and to trust in Jesus Christ. Repentance and faith are like two sides of the same coin. We turn from darkness as we turn to the light.

If you realize this is true, then simply affirm the Gospel message you read above. Repeat the words and verbally say, "*I believe Jesus is the Son of God and God raised Him from the dead on my behalf.*" God hears the simplest of prayers from a sincere heart. These truths can alter your life and put you on a path of deep meaning and purpose.

Now, you can also tell others! In the end it is the highest privilege we have as humans: to offer this grace and mercy to everyone we know, on His behalf.

Keep spreading the news!

Dr. Rice Broocks, Co-Founder, Every Nation Church, NYC

Author of *God's Not Dead, The Human Right,* and *Finding Faith at Ground Zero*

WHEN YOU BELIEVE

by Kenneth Babyface Edmonds and Stephen Lawrence Schwartz

Many nights we prayed
With no proof anyone could hear
In our hearts a hopeful song
We barely understood
Now, we are not afraid
Although we know there's much to fear
We were moving mountains
Long before we knew we could, whoa, yes
There can be miracles
When you believe
Though hope is frail, it's hard to kill
Who knows what miracles you can achieve?
When you believe, somehow you will
You will when you believe...

"Nothing is impossible with God."
The angel Gabriel (Luke 1:37)

"Everything is possible for one who believes."
Jesus of Nazareth (Mark 9:23)

MiraclesInManhattan.NYC

Thank you for reading this book. Serving NYC is our great honor and all proceeds from this book will be dedicated to the New York Initiative, which connects people who desire to serve New York City with exciting opportunities for work and involvement.

If you have been touched by this book, you can help keep the miracles going, through a tax-deductible donation at miraclesinmanhattan.nyc.

We can work together to make a difference in NYC and beyond!

For more information, please contact info@miraclesinmanhattan.nyc

"New York City is arguably the most influential city in the world." Dr. Tim Keller